# The kingdom is opened

## LUKE 12 – 24

by Mike McKinley

thegoodbook
COMPANY

# Luke 12-24 For You

If you are reading *Luke 12-24 For You* alongside this Good Book Guide, here is how the studies in this booklet link to the chapters of *Luke 12-24 For You*:

Study One → Ch 1-2
Study Two → Ch 3-4
Study Three → Ch 5-6
Study Four → Ch 6-7

Study Five → Ch 8-9
Study Six → Ch 10
Study Seven → Ch 11
Study Eight → Ch 12

Find out more about *Luke 12-24 For You* at:
www.thegoodbook.com/for-you

The kingdom is opened
The Good Book Guide to Luke 12–24
© Michael McKinley/The Good Book Company, 2017.
Series Consultants: Tim Chester, Tim Thornborough,
                    Anne Woodcock, Carl Laferton

The Good Book Company
Tel: (US): 866 244 2165
Tel (UK): 0333 123 0880
Email (US): info@thegoodbook.com
Email (UK): info@thegoodbook.co.uk

**Websites**
**North America:** www.thegoodbook.com
**UK:** www.thegoodbook.co.uk
**Australia:** www.thegoodbook.com.au
**New Zealand:** www.thegoodbook.co.nz

ISBN: 9781784981174

Printed in the Czech Republic

# CONTENTS

# Introduction: Good Book Guides

Every Bible-study group is different—yours may take place in a church building, in a home or in a cafe, on a train, over a leisurely mid-morning coffee or squashed into a 30-minute lunch break. Your group may include new Christians, mature Christians, non-Christians, moms and tots, students, businessmen or teens. That's why we've designed these *Good Book Guides* to be flexible for use in many different situations.

Our aim in each session is to uncover the meaning of a passage, and see how it fits into the "big picture" of the Bible. But that can never be the end. We also need to appropriately apply what we have discovered to our lives. Let's take a look at what is included:

⊕ **Talkabout:** Most groups need to "break the ice" at the beginning of a session, and here's the question that will do that. It's designed to get people talking around a subject that will be covered in the course of the Bible study.

⊥ **Investigate:** The Bible text for each session is broken up into manageable chunks, with questions that aim to help you understand what the passage is about. The **Leader's Guide** contains **guidance for questions**, and sometimes ☑ additional "follow-up" questions.

⬚ **Explore more (optional):** These questions will help you connect what you have learned to other parts of the Bible, so you can begin to fit it all together like a jig-saw; or occasionally look at a part of the passage that's not dealt with in detail in the main study.

➔ **Apply:** As you go through a Bible study, you'll keep coming across **apply** sections. These are questions to get the group discussing what the Bible teaching means in practice for you and your church. ☐ **Getting personal** is an opportunity for you to think, plan and pray about the changes that you personally may need to make as a result of what you have learned.

⬆ **Pray:** We want to encourage prayer that is rooted in God's word—in line with his concerns, purposes and promises. So each session ends with an opportunity to review the truths and challenges highlighted by the Bible study, and turn them into prayers of request and thanksgiving.

The **Leader's Guide** and introduction provide historical background information, explanations of the Bible texts for each session, ideas for **optional extra** activities, and guidance on how best to help people uncover the truths of God's word.

# Why study Luke 12-24?

Reading the Gospel of Luke is like climbing a mountain.

The first four chapters take us into the lower foothills, introducing us to Jesus, the promised Savior who will reign on the throne of David as King over God's people, and who announced good news for the poor, oppressed, and needy.

From there, the climb begins in earnest, as Jesus launches his public ministry of healing, exorcism, and teaching, revealing his divine power and explaining both the surprising nature of his kingdom and also what is required of someone who desires to be a citizen of it.

The first major peak in our climb comes in chapter 9, where Peter identifies Jesus as "God's Messiah," only to be told by the Messiah that he will suffer, be killed, and then rise to life three days later. From this point on, everything will be leading us toward Jesus' suffering in Jerusalem: "As the time approached for him to be taken up to heaven, Jesus resolutely set out for Jerusalem" (v 51).

In this Good Book Guide, we join Jesus and the disciples on their long and steady approach toward Jerusalem, over something like a plateau extending from Luke 9 to Luke 19. Along the way, we will encounter some of Jesus' best-known and best-loved parables: stories of incredible love with surprising heroes. We will also see Jesus teaching about the nature of his return and intensifying his preparation for his disciples as the crisis of his crucifixion looms ever larger on the horizon.

In the middle of chapter 19, we find ourselves at the base of a final grand peak—a foreboding cliff that disappears into the clouds. As Jesus enters into Jerusalem, the unthinkable will begin to unfold—the Lord Jesus betrayed, arrested, tried, and crucified. Yet just when the darkness begins to seem overwhelming and our trip seems it might have been a terrible mistake, the clouds give way to the glories of the resurrection and the joy of the disciples in knowing that their Lord is alive forever.

So in these eight studies, Luke will mark out your path to the summit. In turns the climb will be surprising, challenging, reassuring, desperate, and thrilling. Expect to be transformed by Jesus as you see him on the road, follow him to the cross, and meet him beyond the empty tomb, risen and reigning.

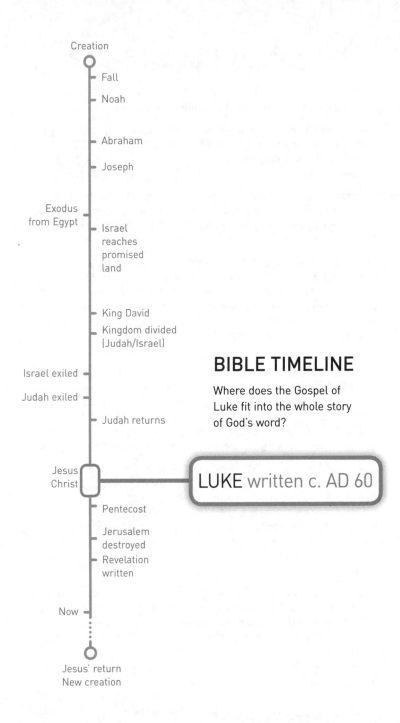

Creation

Fall

Noah

Abraham

Joseph

Exodus
from Egypt

Israel
reaches
promised
land

King David

Kingdom divided
(Judah/Israel)

Israel exiled

Judah exiled

Judah returns

## BIBLE TIMELINE

Where does the Gospel of
Luke fit into the whole story
of God's word?

Jesus
Christ

**LUKE** written c. AD 60

Pentecost

Jerusalem
destroyed

Revelation
written

Now

Jesus' return
New creation

# 1

## Luke 12 v 35 – 14 v 6

# GET READY AND COME IN

## ⊕ talkabout

1. What future events affect your thinking, feelings or actions right now?

## ⊕ investigate

2. What do each of these passages from the first half of Luke tell us about:
   • Jesus the Messiah-King    • Jesus' kingdom    • life as Jesus' subjects?
   • 1 v 30-33


   • 2 v 8-14


   • 4 v 42-44


   • 9 v 20-26


   • 9 v 28-35


   • 11 v 20-23

Toward the end of chapter 9 Luke told us that, "As the time approached for him to be taken up to heaven, Jesus resolutely set out for Jerusalem" (Luke 9:51). The second half of Luke's Gospel unfolds in light of that larger purpose, and each encounter seems to move Jesus closer to his death in Jerusalem. The tone of the second half also shifts noticeably, as Jesus spends more time preparing his disciples for life in the time between his departure and his return in glory and judgment.

> **Read Luke 12 v 35 – 13 v 9**

3. What key piece of information about the future does Jesus give in verse 40?

4. How does the parable in verses 35-48 tell us to live in light of that future day?

## ⊡ explore more

*optional*

*What does Jesus say he has not come to bring, and that he has come to bring (12 v 49, 51)?*
*To what does "fire" refer (see 3 v 9, 17)?*
*How will this be experienced and witnessed now, before the Son of Man returns in glory (12 v 52-53)?*
*What will Jesus undergo before the final fire comes (v 50)?*

In the Old Testament, God's judgment is pictured as a flood of overwhelming water (read Isaiah 8 v 7-8 and Jonah 2 v 3-6). Sometimes, it literally was one (read Genesis 6 v 11-23 and Exodus 14 v 26-30).

*Why is it wonderful news that Jesus went through his "baptism" before he will bring his "fire"?*

**5.** How do these three sections tell us about what to expect of life now?
  - 12 v 49-53

  - 12 v 54-59

  - 13 v 1-9?

  - How do they tell us what to do in life now?
  - 12 v 49-53

  - 12 v 54-59

  - 13 v 1-9?

# ➔ apply

**6.** What difference should the truth of 12 v 40 make to our lives today?

- Which of these is most firmly established in your life? Which are lacking?

## ⊡ getting personal

The eighteenth-century American preacher Jonathan Edwards wrote as a young man, "Resolved, never to do any thing, which I should be afraid to do, if I expected it would not be above an hour, before I should hear the last trump" at the Son of Man's return.

What would change tomorrow if you made the same resolution? How will you ensure you live in light of what you know the future holds?

## ⬇ investigate

### ▶ Read Luke 13 v 10 – 14 v 1-6

Luke bookends the next section with accounts of two miraculous healings.

**7.** When do they take place? And what are the responses to Jesus' actions?

**DICTIONARY**

**Hypocrites (13 v 15):** people who say one thing but do something else.
**Pharisee (14 v 1):** a member of a powerful religious group who took obedience to God's commands extremely seriously—and added many extra rules to ensure they did not break those commands.
**Law (v 3):** God's law in the Old Testament.
**Mustard seed (v 19):** is tiny!
**Abraham, Isaac and Jacob (v 28):** the "patriarchs"—the forefathers of the people of Israel.
**Herod (v 31):** Herod Antipas, the king (under the Romans) of Galilee, in the north of Israel. He had already killed Jesus' relative, John the Baptist (9 v 9).

The Greek text of verse 18 contains the word "therefore," so we should interpret Jesus' words in verses 18-21 in light of the healing that came immediately before it. The demonstration of a power that could deliver the bent-over woman from the power of Satan raised the question that Jesus picks up in verse 18 and verse 20: if Jesus is establishing the kingdom of God, what will it look like? Will it be characterized by spectacular displays of spiritual might and triumphant conquest?

**8.** How do verses 18-21 provide Jesus' answer to that question?

• To what extent does the history of the church bear out Jesus' description of his kingdom, do you think?

**9.** How are verses 22-30 both a promise and a warning?

• Is it easy to reach Christ's eternal kingdom?

**10.** How does Jesus feel about those who reject him (v 34-35)?

## ⊡ getting personal

When Jesus quotes Psalm 118 v 26 in Luke 13 v 35, he is likely referring to his future return in judgment. At that time Jerusalem will have no choice but to acknowledge Jesus as the Lord's King.

The same is true for us—we will either hail Jesus as King now and so enter the great feast through the narrow door, or we will gnash our teeth as we are forced to acknowledge him after the door has shut.

Check your heart. Are you acknowledging Jesus as your King now, and living in light of the future arrival of his kingdom—or not?

## ➔ apply

**11.** How can we use verses 18-21 to encourage ourselves when it does not seem that God is at work in the world around us, or at work through us?

**12.** In what ways should verses 34-35 shape our thinking about and talking with those we know who are not taking refuge under Jesus' wings?

## ↑ pray

**Thank God:**

- that Jesus is coming back, and that he has given you work to do and people to serve as you wait for that future event.
- that his kingdom is growing, and that it includes you.

**Ask God:**

- to show you any ways you are not living now with your future in mind.
- to enable you to let the future coming of Christ shape your perspective on the highs and lows of this life.

# 2 Luke 14 v 7 – 15 v 32
# THE BANQUET AND THE SEARCH

## The story so far

Jesus taught that he will return to bring his kingdom in all its glory, and to save, reward, and judge—and calls his people to stay repentant and keep serving.

## ⊕ talkabout

1. Have you ever rejected an invitation or offer that you later wished you'd accepted?

   - Have you ever ducked a difficult challenge that you later realized you should have taken on?

## ⊕ investigate

▶ **Read Luke 14 v 7-24**

2. What statement does someone eating with Jesus make (v 15)?

**DICTIONARY**

**Exalted (v 11):** raised up.
**Righteous (v 14):** here, meaning those who are in right relationship with God, through faith in Jesus.
**Feast in the kingdom of God (v 15):** Isaiah 25 v 6-9 pictured the coming of God's kingdom as a sumptuous feast.

**3.** Who misses out on that banquet?

&bull; v 7-11

&bull; v 16-20 (Think about what kinds of real-life people the characters in the parable would represent.)

**4.** Who *is* included in the banquet (v 11, 21-23)?

> ❯ **Read Luke 14 v 25-35**

**5.** What is the path to the banquet at Jesus' eternal table like (v 26-27)?

**DICTIONARY**

**Hate (v 26):** a common Hebrew way of speaking, meaning to make something else an absolute priority over the "hated" thing.

**6.** Jesus was being followed by "large crowds" (v 25). Why do you think he chose to tell them the mini-parables of verses 28-32? (Hint: Verse 33 is helpful!)

# ➔ apply

**7.** Think about how you talk about the Christian life to others. How is that similar or different than Jesus' description here?

• If there are differences, why is that? And what effect does that have on people's Christian lives?

## ⊡ getting personal

There is nothing in our lives that we can point to and tell Jesus that it is off-limits.

Is that true of your approach to your Christian life? How have you experienced Jesus strengthening you to follow him wholeheartedly? In what ways do you need to ask him for help to find your identity in knowing him, your cause in serving him, and your joy in obeying him?

## ⊻ investigate

**❯ Read Luke 15 v 1-32**

**8.** How do these two parables explain why Jesus is welcoming and eating with "sinners" (15 v 1-2)?

> **DICTIONARY**
>
> **Repents (v 7):** accepts Jesus' rule instead of living under their own.
> **Pigs (v 15):** to Jews, pigs were unclean animals.

**9.** What did it take to rescue the sheep and find the coin?

• What did the lost sheep and the lost coin contribute to the rescue?

**10.** How is the younger son like the sheep and the coin?

• How is the older son a warning to the Pharisees who were muttering back in verse 2?

⊡ **explore more**

optional

❯ **Read Ezekiel 34 v 2-6**

God has some complaints to make against his shepherds (the leaders of his people, Israel).

*What are they not doing?*

❯ **Read Ezekiel 34 v 11-13**

*What did God promise would happen, and who would achieve this? How have we seen Jesus fulfilling that promise in Luke 15?*

## → apply

**11.** In what way is it easy for committed Christians to become muttering Pharisees? Why is that dangerous?

**12.** How is this insight into what brings heaven joy both a thrill for us and a challenge to us?

## ⊡ getting personal

If your joy is provoked by the same thing that God's is this week, how will that affect:
* your view of, and conversations with, those around you who don't know Jesus?
* your actions toward someone who used to come to your church, but no longer does?
* your prayer life?

## ↑ pray

**Praise God:**

* for the heavenly banquet he has invited people to join him at.
* for coming in the person of his Son to search for you and find you and forgive you.

**Ask God:**

* to shape your heart so that you would find joy where he finds joy.
* to show you ways in which you may have a Pharisee-like view of others.
* to help you be the means by which God seeks and finds the lost who live around you (you might like to pray for specific people).

# 3 Luke 16 v 1 – 18 v 8
# THE KINGDOM IS COMING

## The story so far

Jesus taught that he will return to bring his kingdom in all its glory, and to save, reward, and judge—and calls his people to stay repentant and keep serving.

In a series of parables, Jesus pictures himself as the great seeker, come to rescue sinners. We need to accept the invitation and walk home, even when it's hard.

## ⊕ talkabout

**1.** What stops people becoming Christians, or stops people continuing to live as Christians?

## ⊕ investigate

> **Read Luke 16 v 1-12**

**2.** What does the manager do with his position? Why?

> **DICTIONARY**
>
> **Commended (v 8):** praised.

**3.** What lesson does Jesus draw for his followers, and why (v 8-9)?

> **Read Luke 16 v 13-18**

**4.** What warnings does Jesus give about our attitude toward money here?

## explore more

*optional*

The Pharisees have objected to everything about Jesus' ministry (e.g. 15 v 1-2; 16 v 14). And Jesus has angered and confused them with his approach to the Scriptures: on one hand he seems utterly unconcerned to keep their rules (see 13 v 14-15 and 14 v 1-6), but on the other, he seems to press for an even higher standard of obedience and righteousness for his followers (see Matthew 5 v 20).

> **Re-read Luke 16 v 16-18**

*In what way have things been different since the time of John the Baptist?*
*In what sense are they the same (v 17—see also Matthew 5 v 17-18)?*
*What does Jesus say his followers are to do when it comes to divorce (Luke 16 v 18)?*
*Read Deuteronomy 24 v 1-4 and Genesis 2 v 18-25. Is Jesus' standard higher or lower than that of "the Law and the Prophets"? What does this tell us about Jesus' approach to the law?*

The arrival of the kingdom does not nullify the law, but transforms the hearts of its citizens so that they will long to obey God's will (see Jeremiah 31 v 33).

> **Read Luke 16 v 19-31**

**5.** In what sense is this parable a warning to those who are wealthy?

- In what sense is it a warning to those who have access to clear Bible teaching?

- So how is it a challenge to "the Pharisees, who loved money" (v 14)?

## ⊖ apply

This section invites us to examine our relationship with our money and our possessions. Does our attitude to our wealth, and our generosity with our salary and possessions, reflect a heart that loves God and his ways, or money and what it buys?

**6.** In what ways do you as a church find it easy to excuse loving and serving money as your real Master?

- What would someone who is "kingdom-shrewd" with their wealth look like in your context?

## getting personal

Like the rich man's brothers, we have all of the revelation that we need in the Scriptures. We are not lacking instruction about how we ought to think about money and riches. The only question is whether we are listening.

What aspect of Jesus' teaching here do you need to start listening to?

## investigate

It will be easier to apply the lessons of the opening section of chapter 17 (v 1-19) if we first tackle the more complex teaching that follows it (v 20-37).

> **Read Luke 17 v 20-37**

7.  In what sense was the kingdom of God already "in [their] midst" (v 21), do you think?

*   But what does Jesus also tell his disciples (v 22-25)?

8.  So in what sense had the kingdom already arrived, and in what sense has the kingdom not yet arrived?

**9.** What does Jesus say the future coming of the kingdom will be like (v 26-37)?

So Jesus' followers must wrestle with what it looks like to live now in a way that makes sense of the twin facts that:

1. the kingdom has already come in the person of its King, Jesus.

2. the kingdom has yet to come in all its fullness, when its King returns in power.

> **Read Luke 17 v 1-19; 18 v 1-8**

**10.** What principles for living in this "already/not yet" tension do verses 1-19 give us?

• v 1-3a

• v 3b-4

• v 5-6

• v 7-10

• v 11-19

• 18 v 1-8

⊟ **apply**

**11.** What reasons for failing to start loving, or keep loving, God do these chapters of Luke offer us?

• How do they also offer us the solutions to these reasons?

⬆ **pray**

Use your answers to Questions Six and Twelve to shape your prayers.

# 4 Luke 18 v 9 – 19 v 44
# INS AND OUTS

## The story so far

Jesus taught that he will return to bring his kingdom in all its glory, and to save, reward, and judge—and calls his people to stay repentant and keep serving.

In a series of parables, Jesus pictures himself as the great seeker, come to rescue sinners. We need to accept the invitation and walk home, even when it's hard.

Jesus announced that between his coming as King and return to establish his kingdom, his people are to live under his rule, in light of their future.

## ⊕ talkabout

1. What is necessary for someone to enter God's eternal kingdom?

   • What prevents people from entering his kingdom?

## ⊕ investigate

> **Read Luke 18 v 9-14**

2. What is good about the Pharisee (v 10-12)?

---

**DICTIONARY**

**Justified (v 14):** here, meaning given a verdict of being "not guilty and totally without fault" by God.

---

- How does his prayer reveal his society's attitudes toward tax collectors?

**3.** Why is Jesus' verdict in verse 14 shocking?

- How does it answer the question: who is part of God's kingdom?

> **Read Luke 18 v 15 – 19 v 10**

In each of these episodes, Luke records an interaction between Jesus and an individual or group. In each, we are watching the parable of the Pharisee and the tax collector coming true in reality.

**4.** How do we see the themes of that parable in the approach of each person/group to Jesus; and in the relationship with Jesus they finish the episode with?

- 18 v 15-17

- 18 v 18-25

• 18 v 35-43

• 19 v 1-10

optional

## 🔅 explore more

*Jesus' final words in these episodes reveal that his mission is "to seek and to save the lost" (v 10). Who are the "lost" in these passages?*

**▶ Read Ezekiel 34 v 11-12, 16**

*How does Luke show us Jesus fulfilling this promise in real people's real lives?*

## 😊 getting personal

Jesus' love transforms people and sets them free to love him back; it was so for the blind man and Zacchaeus, and it is so today.

How has Jesus' love transformed you? How will it go on transforming you? And when was the last time you stopped to marvel at his love for you, and give thanks for his mercy to you?

**5.** How does 18 v 27-33 answer the following questions?
   • "Who then can be saved?" (v 26)

• Is it worth leaving everything to follow Jesus?

## ⇥ apply

**6.** What would the attitudes and decisions of the children, the blind beggar and Zacchaeus look like in your own life?

• What would the attitude and decisions of the rich young ruler look like in your own life?

**7.** What are the danger signs that someone is approaching Jesus like the Pharisee in the parable, rather than the tax collector?

## ⤓ investigate

### ▶ Read Luke 19 v 11-27

This parable contains two different stories, one about a nobleman and his interaction with his subjects (19 v 12, 14, 27), and also a more detailed story about that nobleman's interaction with his servants, to whom he had given some money to invest.

**8.** How does the parable about the nobleman and his subjects warn those who are not submitting to Jesus as King?

**9.** How does the parable about the nobleman and his servants encourage and warn those who are submitting to him?

⊡ **getting personal**

The place where you live, the job where you work, your weekends, the abilities and education that you have received, your money, your health, your family, your interactions with people who do not believe in Jesus, your suffering—all of it is given to you as a stewardship.

Do you steward those things as a servant who will one day give an account to your King? Are you failing to use them in the interests of your Master in any way?

▶ **Read Luke 19 v 28-44**

Just as the parable introduced us to a would-be king, Jesus approaches Jerusalem as "the king who comes in the name of the Lord" (v 38). His decision to ride a colt is an intentional fulfillment of prophecy...

| DICTIONARY |
| --- |
| **Colt (v 30):** male donkey or horse. |

**10.** **Read Zechariah 9 v 9-10.** What is Jesus claiming:

• about who he is?

• about what he is like?

• about what he will do?

**11.** How do those present respond to his claims?

• How does Jesus reveal the importance of the choice of how we respond (v 41-44)?

## ⤳ apply

**12.** If we look at the world around us in the way Jesus looked at Jerusalem in verses 41-44, what would we...

• feel?

• say?

• Does this describe the way you look at those around you who do not submit to Jesus as King? Why / why not?

## ⤒ pray

Speak to your King, confessing your sins and your ongoing need for mercy, and your ongoing need of help to give him first place in your life. Thank him that those who give up much get far more back.

# 5 Luke 19 v 45 – 21 v 38
# SHOWDOWN AT THE TEMPLE

## The story so far

Jesus taught that he will return to bring his kingdom in all its glory—and calls his people to live in light of their future in their priorities and actions.

In a series of parables, Jesus pictures himself as the great seeker, come to rescue sinners. We need to accept the invitation and walk home, even when it's hard.

Jesus' interactions with a great variety of people reveal that the humble who come with empty hands find life; those who approach proudly leave without life.

## ⊕ talkabout

1. Does intelligence, success or education help or hinder us in our efforts to understand the Bible, do you think? Why?

## ⊕ investigate

Since 9 v 51, Jesus has been walking towards Jerusalem and then being "taken up to heaven"—now he has entered the city. The next two chapters take place in the temple complex. As it was the center of the Jewish religious life of which Jesus has been so critical, it is fitting that the final showdowns of his earthly ministry take place here at the temple.

> **DICTIONARY**
> **Vineyard (20 v 9):** an Old Testament image for Israel.
> **Cornerstone (v 17):** the first, most important stone in a building.
> **Caesar (v 22):** the Roman Emperor.
> **Duplicity (v 23):** deceit.

❯ **Read Luke 19 v 45 – 20 v 26**

2. What is the aim of the chief priests, teachers of the law, and people's leaders (19 v 47)? What is their problem (v 48)?

So the religious leaders try to trap Jesus verbally into saying something that will either cause the crowd to turn against him or the Roman authorities to arrest him…

**3.** What is their first question (20 v 2)? Why is it a clever one to ask?

- What is even cleverer about Jesus' answer (v 3-4—v 5-6 will help)?

- The leaders had been trying to show up the weakness of Jesus' position, but how does Jesus wind up showing the weakness of theirs?

**4.** What is their second question (v 22)? Why is it a clever one to ask?

- What is even cleverer about Jesus' answer (v 24-25)?

• How does Jesus here show us the Christian view of how we relate to authorities?

**▶ Read Luke 20 v 27 – 21 v 4**

**5.** Who asks the third question, and what is it (20 v 27-33)? Why is it a clever one to ask?

• How does Jesus answer (v 34-38)?

• How does Jesus here show us part of the Christian view of marriage?

## ⊡ explore more

*Who asks the question that initiates the fourth discussion (20 v 41)? What is the answer to the question of verse 44?*

**6.** How does Jesus' parable in verses 9-16 provide his assessment of what is really going on?

• What is tragically ironic about the response of the teachers of the law and the chief priests to the parable (v 19)?

**7.** Compare 19 v 45-46 and 20 v 45-47 with 21 v 1-4. What religious approaches does Jesus criticize, and what religious approach does he praise?

### ⊡ getting personal

The widow's gift was actually accounted by Jesus as "more than all the others" (v 3) because instead of giving out of her excess and wealth, she gave (literally in the Greek) "all her life."

How does this encourage or comfort you, as you look at your own life?

Is there an area of your life where you are giving nothing to God, or just enough to look good before others? What would it mean to give all you have?

# → apply

**8.** Sum up what you have learned about:

• the life of true discipleship that pleases Jesus.

• the life of false religion that Jesus opposes.

• Why is it challenging that Jesus' greatest opponents were the most religious people around him?

# ↓ investigate

Luke 21 v 5-38 marks the conclusion of Jesus' public ministry. Its predictions of destruction alternate between the near horizon and things that will happen in the future—between the events of AD 70, when Jerusalem and its temple were destroyed by Roman armies, and the triumphant return and the end of this world as we know it. Keeping that alternation in mind solves a lot of the passage's difficulties.

We are positioned in history between the events that Jesus describes; we look back to AD 70, and forward to the day when Jesus will return.

**❯ Read Luke 21 v 5-38**

**9.** Which parts of v 8-36 do you think describe the events of AD 70, and which the events of Jesus' return, which still lies in the future? Which seem unclear?

> **DICTIONARY**
>
> **Adversaries (v 15):** opponents.
> **Redemption (v 28):** here, freedom.

**10.** What does Jesus want his followers to:

• watch out for (v 8-9)?

• make up their minds about (v 12-19)?

• look forward to (v 25-28)?

• be careful about (v 34)?

• pray for (v 36)?

## ⊖ apply

**11.** Looking through your answers to Question Ten, how can you help each other to do each of these things? What might cause you not to do them?

## ⊡ getting personal

The two things that are promised in this passage are future suffering and future triumph. So Jesus tells you to "stand up and lift up your heads, because your redemption is drawing near" (v 28)?

How does this thought excite you? How does it comfort you? How does it help you to worry less about today, and focus more on your future?

## ⬆ pray

Use your responses to the Getting Personal section above to fuel your praise and your requests.

# 6

## Luke 9 v 1-62
# THE NIGHT OF TRIALS

*The story so far*

Jesus taught that he will return to bring his kingdom in all its glory—but first, he has come as the great seeker, to rescue the lost and bring them home.

Jesus' interactions with a great variety of people reveal that the humble who come with empty hands find life; those who approach proudly leave without life.

In Jerusalem, Jesus faced verbal assaults, but out-argued his enemies while pointing to a poor yet generous widow as an example of a God-pleasing life.

## ⊕ talkabout

1. Have you ever stood up for someone, or for the truth, even though you knew it was risky? What caused you to take that stand?

• Have you ever let someone down badly? What caused you to do so? Were you able to repair the relationship—and if so, how?

## ⊕ investigate

All the action now takes place during the Passover and the accompanying Feast of Unleavened Bread. Jerusalem was thronged with visitors, there to commemorate and celebrate God's deliverance of his people from Egypt through the death of the sacrificed lambs (Exodus 12 v 1-20).

**▶ Read Luke 22 v 1-38**

**2.** What is shocking about:
  - Judas' actions (v 4-6)?

**DICTIONARY**

**Covenant (v 20):** binding agreement or promise.
**Decreed (v 22):** decided; ordered.
**Woe (v 22):** judgment; condemnation.
**Confer on (v 29):** give.
**Simon (v 31):** Peter's birth name.
**Transgressors (v 37):** law-breakers.

  - Jesus' words about the Passover meal (v 14-20)?

  - the disciples' priorities (v 24)?

  - Jesus' statements about Peter and about himself (v 31-37)?

**3.** What do verses 25-26 teach us about a Christian view of greatness?

  - How do the example of Jesus (v 27) and the gift of Jesus (v 29-30) help us to obey this teaching of Jesus?

The world may be motivated by personal glory—Jesus' followers are "not to be like that" (v 26).

How might you be in danger of using an area of influence or position of leadership "like that"? What would it look like to use it to serve like Jesus? Will you do so?

▶ **Read Luke 22 v 39-46**

4.  **Read Isaiah 51 v 17 and Jeremiah 25 v 15-16.** What is "the cup" (Luke 22 v 42) that Jesus asks his Father to remove?

    • What is astonishing about the second half of verse 42?

5.  How do verses 41-44 make you feel?

➔ **apply**

6.  How does the account of Jesus on the Mount of Olives show you:
    • what love is?

• how loved Jesus' people are?

## ⬇ investigate

> **Read Luke 22 v 47-71**

**7.** Who mistreats Jesus in these harrowing scenes? How?

**DICTIONARY**

**Asserted (v 59):**
claimed; argued.
**Testimony (v 71):**
spoken evidence.

**8.** What does Peter claim about himself (v 55-60)?

• What does Jesus claim about himself (v 69-70—see Daniel 7 v 13-14)?

**9.** Who is really on trial in all these overnight events?

• Who ends their trial with their credibility intact? Who loses theirs?

## ⊡ explore more

> ❯ **Read Philippians 2 v 6-11**

These verses are a timeline of the incarnation, death, ascension and exaltation of the eternal Son of God.

*Where on that timeline do the events of Luke 22 take place?*
*What is to follow (Philippians 2 v 8-11)?*
*Who will recognize Jesus as Lord at the final trial at Christ's return?*
*How do you think knowing this truth, as he did (Luke 22 v 69), strengthened Jesus to tell the truth at his trial and walk toward death on his cross?*

**10.** Do you think Simon Peter overreacts to his failures in verses 61-62? Why / why not?

• Why is there still hope for him (v 32—see 24 v 33-36)?

## ⊟ apply

**11.** What difference would it make to Jesus' identity if no one in the world believes he is the Son of Man?

• How should that affect how we live in this world?

**12.** How has reading about the events of the night before Jesus' death motivated you to be publicly loyal to him?

### ⊡ getting personal

Because Jesus died for his people's sins, there is mercy and forgiveness for everyone who falls and fails. When you sin, do not run from Jesus; run to him!

Are you doing this in response to your sin?

Is there a sin that you have sought to hide, make up for, or excuse, that you need to weep about and cry for forgiveness for?

Remember that Jesus knew you would sin in that way—and he chose to suffer the agony of God's judgment for it anyway. "If anybody does sin, we have an advocate with the Father—Jesus Christ, the Righteous One. He is the atoning sacrifice for our sins" (1 John 2 v 1-2).

### ⊡ pray

If the Getting Personal section above has prompted you to repent properly and enjoy receiving God's forgiveness, take time to speak to him about this now.

**Re-read verses 39-44**, and thank your Savior for all that he went through on your behalf so that you might drink the cup at God's eternal banquet instead of the cup of his wrath.

# 7 Luke 23 v 1-47
# OPENING THE KINGDOM

## The story so far

Jesus' interactions with a great variety of people revealed that the humble who come with empty hands find life; those who approach proudly leave without life.

In Jerusalem, Jesus faced verbal assaults, out-arguing his enemies while pointing to a poor-yet-generous widow as an example of the life that pleases God.

The night before he died, Jesus was betrayed, deserted, denied and mocked; but he continued to stand for truth and walk towards the horror of the cross.

## ⊕ talkabout

1. What would you say are the most important turning points in history?

## ⊌ investigate

> **Read Luke 23 v 1-31**

2. What does Pilate know (v 4, 15, 22)?

• What does Pilate do (v 24-25)? Why, do you think?

**DICTIONARY**

**Pilate (v 1):** Pontius Pilate, the Roman governor of Judea.
**Subverting (v 1):** undermining; working against.
**Jurisdiction (v 7):** area of authority.
**Insurrection (v 19):** rebellion.
**Prevailed (v 23):** proved most powerful.
**Cyrene (v 26):** a city in modern-day Libya.

**3.** How does the crowd respond to Pilate's desire to release Jesus (v 18, 21, 23)?

• Who would they rather have as part of their society than the Lord Jesus (v 18-19)?

**4.** What did Barabbas face at the start of the day, and at the end of the day? Why?

## ⊡ explore more

optional

*When the women following Jesus mourned for him, what did Jesus tell them to do (v 28)?*
*Why should they do this (v 29-30)?*

In verse 30, Jesus quotes to the ladies from Hosea 10 v 8, a prophecy that was realized when the Assyrian armies overran the northern kingdom of Israel in 722 BC.

**▶ Read Luke 21 v 20-24**

What is Jesus saying the women should save their mourning for?

**▶ Read Revelation 6 v 12-17**

*What else is Jesus telling them to save their mourning for?*

## ⊟ apply

**5.** How do we see the crowd's decision being made in our own lives, and in our society?

> • **Read 1 Peter 3 v 18; Colossians 2 v 21-22; Revelation 1 v 5b.** How are we like Barabbas?

## ⊡ investigate

### ❯ Read Luke 23 v 32-47

**6.** How do the two criminals crucified with Jesus respond to him?

• v 39

**DICTIONARY**

**Casting lots (v 34):** throwing dice.
**Remember (v 42):** i.e. act in my interest; help me.
**Centurion (v 47):** most likely he was the soldier in charge of Jesus' execution.

• v 40-42

Remember, these men are "both criminals" (v 32)—their crimes are serious enough to bring a verdict of execution, as the second criminal himself acknowledges (v 41).

**7.** So what is remarkable about Jesus' words in verse 43?

• In what sense are the words "with me" the most exciting part of this promise?

## getting personal

Ask yourself, could you be happy in heaven, free from suffering and sadness, even if Jesus was not there? What would satisfy you, short of Jesus? What other pleasures are enough, that you could be satisfied with them for all eternity?

Look at Jesus. Look at his love for you, what he went through for you, the future he has secured for you... Look at his honesty, humility, integrity, sacrifice... and "with me" will become the most precious words in your life.

**8.** **Read Joel 2 v 1-2 and Amos 5 v 18-20.** What does the darkness in the middle of the day (Luke 23 v 44-45) signify?

**9.** What two things happen in the darkness?
• v 45

• v 46

10. **Read Genesis 3 v 23-24 and Exodus 26 v 30-34.** What did the curtain in the temple represent?

11. Explain what Jesus' death achieved, using the events of verses 44-45a, 45b, and 46.

⊡ **getting personal**

The centurion, a Gentile executioner, saw "what had happened" and was led to praise God and declare Jesus' innocence (v 47). Through Luke, you see what that centurion saw.

Is your response to praise God? How does this reveal itself in your life?

⊡ **apply**

12. How will Christians view death, and why?

## ⊡ **pray**

Choose a verse, or a conversation, in this passage and praise Jesus for what you see of his character and his compassion there.

# 8

## Luke 23 v 48 – 24 v 53
# REMEMBER HOW HE TOLD YOU

*The story so far*

In Jerusalem, Jesus faced verbal assaults, out-arguing his enemies while pointing to a poor-yet-generous widow as an example of the life that pleases God.

The night before he died, Jesus was betrayed, deserted, denied and mocked; but he continued to stand for truth and walk towards the horror of the cross.

The death of Christ opened the way into his kingdom for absolutely anyone by bearing God's judgment in their place. Death holds no fear for Jesus' subjects.

## ⊕ talkabout

**1.** What has been the greatest positive surprise of your life?

• Did that positive surprise change the way you were feeling in any way? How?

## ⊕ investigate

The events surrounding Jesus' crucifixion may be familiar to us, but you can easily imagine the confusion that they left in the minds of those who had known him....

▶ **Read Luke 23 v 48-55**

**DICTIONARY**

**Beat their breasts (v 48):** a sign of mourning or sadness.
**Council (v 50):** see 22 v 66.

**2.** How do the women (v 49, 55-56) and Joseph (v 50-54) give us a picture of what real discipleship involves?

> **Read Luke 24 v 1-8**

**3.** What facts confront the women (v 2-3)?

- Who provides an explanation for those facts (v 4-5)? What is that explanation (v 5-6)?

**4.** In a sense the women should not have been surprised by what they have found. Why not (v 6-7)?

**5.** What does the empty tomb tell them, and us, about Jesus' promises?

What the women needed to do most in order to make sense of what had happened was to remember what Jesus had already said (v 6, 8). While we are obviously not in the same situation as these women, we too will most likely face times when our lives do not make sense. In these moments, we need to remember the things that Jesus has said to us about what it will mean for us to live as his disciples.

**6.** What has Jesus promised us?
- 6 v 22-23

- 9 v 24

- 11 v 13

- 11 v 28

- 12 v 4-8

- 12 v 40; 17 v 22-24

- 18 v 29-30

## ⊡ apply

**7.** Which of these promises do you find hardest to believe and act upon? How does trusting it give greater joy and security in life?

## ⊡ getting personal

"Remember how he told you..." You can be sure that Jesus has told you everything that you need to know in order to live faithfully in your situation, in your day.

Is there a particular time or situation in which you will particularly need to remember one of these promises from your Lord? How will you make sure you call it to mind?

# ⬇ investigate

**❯ Read Luke 24 v 9-12**

It is easy to imagine how excited these women were to tell everyone the good news that would turn their sadness into celebration (v 9). But the reaction of the disciples is like a bucket of cold water being poured on the proceedings: "their words seemed to them like nonsense" (v 11).

Peter went to investigate for himself (v 12), but without the angelic interpreters, he could only wonder to himself about the meaning of the "strips of linen lying by themselves."

**❯ Read Luke 24 v 13-53**

8. What does Jesus do to change their minds about the claims of the women (v 13-45)?

> **DICTIONARY**
>
> **The Scriptures (v 27):** here, meaning the Old Testament.
> **Peace (v 36):** shalom; the experience of wholeness and harmony, enjoying relationship with God.
> **In his name (v 47):** by his authority; that is, it is him who makes these things possible.
> **Power from on high (v 49):** the Holy Spirit.

9. Why are Jesus' first words to his gathered disciples in verse 36 surprising, and wonderful? (Hint: think about the disciples' performance over the previous few days.)

10. We do not have the risen Jesus standing in front of us, but we do have the Scriptures, including Moses and all the prophets. Why is this wonderful for us (v 25-27, 44-49)?

**11.** What is the mission of the church (v 47-49, 52-53)?

optional

### ⊡ explore more

*How do the events of the end of Luke's Gospel remind us of the events of the beginning of Luke's Gospel?*

**Read 1 v 8-13, 26-28 and 2 v 8-9; link to 24 v 4-5**
**Read 1 v 7, 13, 31, 34; link to 24 v 1, 3, 5-6**
**Read 1 v 37; link to 24 v 6b-8**
**Read 1 v 46-47 and 2 v 8-10; link to 24 v 52-53**
**Read 2 v 8-11; link to 24 v 46-47**

### ⊡ getting personal

With Jesus enthroned in heaven and the Holy Spirit indwelling the church, the gospel news that Jesus is the suffering Savior who offers forgiveness and the risen Lord who commands repentance can, and must, be spread to all nations.

What part are you going to play in that mission in the next month:
- with your prayers?
- with your finances?
- with your deeds?
- with your words?

Be practical!

### ⊡ apply

**12.** How has Luke's Gospel prompted you to worship Jesus with great joy? Which truths and insights from Luke 12 – 24 have particularly struck you?

## ⬆ **pray**

Use your answers to Question 12 to praise God for his Son, your King. Pray for ever-increasing in the truth of the resurrection and the reliability of Jesus' promises. Speak to him about particular situations in which, or times when, you find such reliance hard.

Finish by praising God joyfully that your King who died for you is now reigning in heaven.

# The kingdom
# is opened
## LEADER'S GUIDE

# Leader's Guide: Luke 12 – 24

## INTRODUCTION

Leading a Bible study can be a bit like herding cats—everyone has a different idea of what the passage could be about, and a different line of enquiry that they want to pursue. But a good group leader is more than someone who just referees this kind of discussion. You will want to:

- correctly understand and handle the Bible passage. But also...

- encourage and train the people in your group to do this for themselves. Don't fall into the trap of spoon-feeding people by simply passing on the information in the Leader's Guide. Then...

- make sure that no Bible study is finished without everyone knowing how the passage is relevant for them. What changes do you all need to make in the light of the things you have been learning? And finally...

- encourage the group to turn all that has been learned and discussed into prayer.

Your Bible-study group is unique, and you are likely to know better than anyone the capabilities, backgrounds and circumstances of the people you are leading. That's why we've designed these guides with a number of optional features. If they're a quiet bunch, you might want to spend longer on *talkabout*. If your time is limited, you can choose to skip *explore more*, or get people to look at these questions at home. Can't get enough of Bible study? Well, some studies have optional extra homework projects. As leader, you can adapt and select the material to the needs of your particular group.

So what's in the Leader's Guide? The main thing that this Leader's Guide will help you to do is to understand the major teaching points in the passage you are studying, and how to apply them. As well as guidance for the questions, the Leader's Guide for each session contains the following important sections:

## THE BIG IDEA

One or two key sentences will give you the main point of the session. This is what you should be aiming to have fixed in people's minds as they leave the Bible study. And it's the point you need to head back toward when the discussion goes off at a tangent.

## SUMMARY

An overview of the passage, including plenty of useful historical background information.

## OPTIONAL EXTRA

Usually this is an introductory activity that ties in with the main theme of the Bible study, and is designed to "break the ice" at the beginning of a session. Or it may be a "homework project" that people can tackle during the week.

So let's take a look at the various different features of a Good Book Guide:

## ⊕ talkabout

Each session kicks off with a discussion question, based on the group's opinions or experiences. It's designed to get people talking and thinking in a general way about the main subject of the Bible study.

# ⬇ investigate

The first thing you and your group need to know is what the Bible passage is about, which is the purpose of these questions. But watch out—people may come up with answers based on their experiences or teaching they have heard in the past, without referring to the passage at all. It's amazing how often we can get through a Bible study without actually looking at the Bible! If you're stuck for an answer, the Leader's Guide contains guidance for questions. These are the answers to direct your group to. This information isn't meant to be read out to people—ideally, you want them to discover these answers from the Bible for themselves. Sometimes there are optional follow-up questions (see ☑ in guidance for questions) to help you help your group get to the answer.

# ⬛ explore more

These questions generally point people to other relevant parts of the Bible. They are useful for helping your group to see how the passage fits into the "big picture" of the whole Bible. These sections are OPTIONAL—only use them if you have time. Remember that it's better to finish in good time having really grasped one big thing from the passage, than to try and cram everything in.

# ➔ apply

We want to encourage you to spend more time working at application—too often, it is simply tacked on at the end. In the Good Book Guides, apply sections are mixed in with the investigate sections of the study. We hope that people will realize that application is not just an optional extra, but rather, the whole purpose of studying the

Bible. We do Bible study so that our lives can be changed by what we hear from God's word. If you skip the application, the Bible study hasn't achieved its purpose.

These questions draw out practical lessons that we can all learn from the Bible passage. You can review what has been learned so far, and think about practical differences that this should make in our churches and our lives. The group gets the opportunity to talk about what they personally have learned.

# ⊡ getting personal

These can be done at home, but it is well worth allowing a few moments of quiet reflection during the study for each person to think and pray about specific changes they need to make in their own lives. Why not have a time for reporting back at the beginning of the following session, so that everyone can be encouraged and challenged by one another to make application a priority?

# ⬆ pray

In Acts 4 v 25-30 the first Christians quoted Psalm 2 as they prayed in response to the persecution of the apostles by the Jewish religious leaders. Today however, it's not as common for Christians to base prayers on the truths of God's word as it once was. As a result, our prayers tend to be weak, superficial and self-centered rather than bold, visionary and God-centered.

The prayer section is based on what has been learned from the Bible passage. How different our prayer times would be if we were genuinely responding to what God has said to us through his word.

# 1

Luke 12 v 35 – 14 v 6

# GET READY AND COME IN

## THE BIG IDEA

In the future the Son of Man will return to bring his kingdom in all its glory: to save, reward and to judge—so we live in light of that reality, first by repenting and then by keeping going and keeping serving.

## SUMMARY

In this passage we find Jesus addressing his disciples, and in 12 v 40 he gives them a key piece of information about the future: the Son of Man will come at an hour when you do not expect him. Jesus often referred to himself as "the Son of Man" (e.g. 5 v 24; 7 v 34), a term that echoed an Old Testament vision of end-time glory and authority found in Daniel 7 v 13-14. Here Jesus describes a day when his crucifixion, resurrection, and ascension into heaven will be in the past and he will return to earth. And in the brief teachings about masters and servants that surround 12 v 40, Jesus makes it clear that when he returns, it will be in order to bring judgment—blessings for the faithful and punishment for the unfaithful.

In the meantime, God's kingdom will grow, not through spectacular means but simply, inexorably and often unseen (13 v 18-21). Jesus promises that anyone can enter that kingdom and enjoy it forever (v 22-30)—but he also warns that the door is narrow. No one comes into the kingdom by accident.

## OPTIONAL EXTRA

These studies begin halfway through Luke, with Jesus on the road to Jerusalem. To introduce your group to what has happened up to 9 v 51, when Jesus sets out for the capital city, download "Read Scripture Luke

1–9 Video" from thebibleproject.com.

## GUIDANCE FOR QUESTIONS

**1. What future events affect your thinking, feelings or actions right now?** These will range from the short-term and mundane—I need to wear smart clothes for work tomorrow so I will iron a shirt now—to more long-term or exciting—I am going on holiday next month so I feel joyful now / I would like to retire one day, so I need to set up a pension scheme now.

The point to make is that everyone plans their actions in the present based on what they believe the future is likely to hold.

**2. What do each of these passages from the first half of Luke tell us about:**
**• Jesus the Messiah-King • Jesus' kingdom • life as Jesus' subjects?** This question helps your group understand, or recap, what the first twelve chapters of the Gospel taught. (If you have moved to this Good Book Guide straight out of *Luke 1–12: Kingdom Come*, you could skip this question). Not every passage will teach about each of the three aspects.

- **1 v 30-33:** The Messiah will reign forever, on David's throne, as the fulfillment of God's promises. His kingdom will therefore never end.

- **2 v 8-14:** The Messiah is both Lord (God) and Savior (rescuer). Jesus' subjects (those on whom God's favor rests) enjoy peace.

- **4 v 42-44:** Jesus was sent to "proclaim the good news of the kingdom of God."

- **9 v 20-26:** Jesus is not merely a prophet, but rather, the Messiah. The Messiah will

58 **LEADER'S GUIDE** | The kingdom is opened

be rejected and killed, but then rise again. Living as a subject of Jesus will involve similar rejection, and even death. At the very least, it will be a daily denying of self-rule and self-centeredness.

- **9 v 28-35:** Jesus, the Messiah, is God's glorious Son. Jesus' subjects must listen to him.

- **11 v 20-23:** The proof of the coming of God's kingdom is Jesus' powerful work in driving out Satan and his demons. He has come as the "stronger" man, overpowering the devil.

**3. What key piece of information about the future does Jesus give in verse 40?** The Son of Man—Jesus—will come at an hour when you do not expect him. Jesus is coming back to this world, and we do not know the day.

**4. How does the parable tell us to live in light of that future day?** Jesus makes it clear that when he returns, it will be in order to bring judgment—blessings for the faithful and punishment for the unfaithful.

- **v 36-38:** In the parable, the master returns and "catches" some of his servants awake and waiting for him. The fact that they are keeping watch testifies to their loyalty. They receive a most unusual reward—the master himself assumes the position of servant, seats them at his table, and waits upon them. So we are to be ready, waiting and watching, because every day is a day that could be the day of our Master's return.

- **v 42-44:** Here, the focus is on the "manager." He should look after those under his care, rather than taking advantage of them. So, we are to care for each other in the ways God has given us to, whether as pastors or fellow church

members. And we are to take care not to "use" others for our own ends, particularly those under our care in some way.

**EXPLORE MORE**
**What does Jesus say he has not come to bring, and that he has come to bring (12 v 49, 51)?** He has not come to bring peace (v 51). He has come to bring "fire" (v 49) and division (v 51). Don't miss the force of these words!
**To what does "fire" refer (see 3 v 9, 17)?** John the Baptist had used this image of fire to speak of the coming judgment and the purging of evil. Most likely, it is this end-time fire that Jesus longs to kindle, because it will establish God's kingdom in a final, full way.
**How will this be experienced and witnessed now, before the Son of Man returns in glory (12 v 52-53)?** We can say that the division that Jesus speaks of in verses 51-53—that split which will naturally occur between those who receive the message of Jesus with joy and those who reject him—amounts to a preliminary experience of that end-time fire. The division demonstrates who are the faithful servants and who will be taken away in the fire of end-time judgment. The new spiritual distinction between people, caused by the coming of Jesus as King, will result even in opposition within families.
**What will Jesus undergo before the final fire comes (v 50)?** "Baptism." This cannot refer to his actual baptism in water, since that took place back in 3 v 21-22. It is a way of describing God's judgment (see note in Explore More on page 8).
**Why is it wonderful news that Jesus went through his "baptism" before he will bring his "fire"?** Because Jesus "baptism" refers to his going through the flood of God's judgment on the cross. He has experienced God's judgment before

the end-time final judgment, so that those who receive him in faith do not need to. His baptism means that we do not have to face his fire.

**5. How do these three sections here tell us about:**
- **what to expect of life now?**
- **12 v 49-53:** It will involve painful division. If we would be faithful to Jesus, we must be willing to embrace the separation it brings. We may have to pay a very high price in order to follow him, including within our own families.
- **12 v 54-59:** Now is the "time" between Jesus coming to bring the kingdom and open the kingdom, and Jesus returning to judge and bring his kingdom fully.
- **13 v 1-9:** Life now does not last forever—it ends with death. The manner of someone's death is not necessarily a verdict on their sinfulness—but the fact of death is a verdict on humanity's sinfulness. Now is a time of God's patience (v 8-9), where he waits to see what kind of "fruit" each of us will grow.
  **Note:** the fig tree was a picture of Israel (e.g. Joel 1 v 7) and the initial warning was directed at those who were members of Israel. But Jesus' warning here applies to us as well.

- **what to do in life now?**
- **12 v 49-53:** Accept the cost and pain involved in following Jesus, who underwent "baptism" in his death on your behalf.
- **12 v 54-59:** Be reconciled to God (the ultimate judge) before it is too late. Sin leaves each of us with a debt toward God that we cannot repay (see the imagery of 7 v 41-49). But the coming of Jesus signifies that we are in a time when we can still be reconciled to God through him.

- **13 v 1-9:** Again, the point is the urgency of repenting before it is too late when Jesus has returned or we have died.

**6. APPLY: What difference should the truth of 12 v 40 make to our lives today?** If you have time, look back at 12 v 4-34, which forms part of Jesus' teaching that continues to 13 v 9. You can then pick out these ways in which we will live if we do believe that the Son of Man will come on a day we do not know and cannot predict:
- 12 v 5: We will "fear" (live in awe of) God more than of man.
- v 8-9: We will witness boldly.
- v 33: We will be radically generous.
- v 42-43: We will care for fellow believers.
- v 58: We will make sure we are reconciled to God, and go on being reconciled to God when we sin.
- 13 v 5: We will repent because we know one day we must die; and we will call others to do the same.

- **Which of these is most firmly established in your life? Which are lacking?** Let this question be both encouraging and challenging. It is good to see where the Lord is at work in us to enable us to "live ready," as well as seeing those areas where we need to ask the Spirit to go to work. You might like to stop at this point (or after the Getting Personal section straight after) to pray for one another.

**7. When do they [the healings in 13 v 10-17; 14 v 1-6] take place?** Both take place on the Sabbath (13 v 10; 14 v 1), a day when the people of Israel had been instructed by the LORD to rest from their labors to remind them of their dependence on and trust in him. **And what are the responses to Jesus' actions?**
- Indignation (13 v 14)—the synagogue

leader thought that such healings should not happen on a day that was designed to show people they needed to depend upon God!

- Delight (v 17).

- Silence (almost certainly an angry silence—14 v 4, 6): Jesus points out that the religious leaders will help their own animals on the Sabbath, but wish to refuse help to those who require healing or spiritual release.

**8. How do verses 18-21 provide Jesus' answer to that question [what will the kingdom of God look like?]?** It does not tend to grow in impressive, spectacular ways. But it does grow. Give it time, and (like yeast and a seed) it will change and transform everything.

- **To what extent does the history of the church bear out Jesus' description of his kingdom, do you think?** In the book of Acts we see a small band of disciples grow to the point where people from every nation on earth are able to "perch in its branches." The message about Jesus spreads slowly but inexorably until it has reached every part of the map, leavening the entire lump of the world. The very existence of our faith, separated as we are from Jesus' earthly ministry by great distance and time, gives evidence for what Jesus is teaching here in Luke 13.

**9. How are verses 22-30 both a promise and a warning?**

- *The promise:* There is a narrow door that leads into God's house (v 24-25)—into the feast of the kingdom of God (v 28-29). And anyone can come in through that door (v 29).

- *The challenge:* (1) The door is narrow. Contrary to the common religious pluralism of our day that likes to imagine that the many religions of the world represent different paths to same salvation, Jesus teaches that the only way in to salvation is through a proper response to him and his teaching.

(2) The door will close. Now is a time when people can enter the kingdom, but that time will end when the Son of Man returns—which could be any day (12 v 40).

(3) There will be surprising people inside the house, and left outside it. Jesus warns his listeners—Jews, who would have found it easy subconsciously to place their confidence in their descent from Abraham, Isaac, and Jacob—that the people of God are not those born into certain families or nations, but those who repent and recognize Jesus as King.

- **Is it easy to reach Christ's eternal kingdom?** No—we must "make every effort" to enter through the narrow door. No one passes through it accidentally or casually or easily. We must invest all of our energy in making sure that we are through that door before it is too late. We should not misunderstand Jesus as saying that we must strive to pile up good works that will merit passage through the door. The point is that we must keep up our effort to listen to him, trust him, and respond to him.

**10. How does Jesus feel about those who reject him (v 34-35)?** He mourns. He knows they will face judgment, just as he warns Jerusalem here—but he takes no delight in that judgment. Read 19 v 41— Jesus weeps over the lost, who will not return to seek refuge and safety with him.

**11. APPLY: How can we use verses 18-21 to encourage ourselves when it does not seem that God is at work in the world around us, or at work through us?** When we share the gospel but do not see immediate fruit, we have to remember that God works in his own ways and in his own timing (see 1 Corinthians 3:6-7). When our churches and our daily lives seem ordinary and unspectacular, we should take comfort from the lesson of the mustard seed—God does not often work in ways that seem impressive at the beginning. We can continue being faithful, knowing that God is in no hurry and that he is content to build patiently and slowly.

**12. APPLY: In what ways should verses 34-35 shape our thinking about and talking with those who are not taking refuge under Jesus' wings?**

- We need to seek to show them and tell them how wonderful it is that Jesus is ready to gather them under his wings, and love them as a mother loves her children.
- We need to be willing to warn them that, outside of refuge in Christ, there is judgment.
- We need to love them enough to care that they will face judgment, and weep about it.

# 2 Luke 14 v 7 – 15 v 32
# THE BANQUET AND THE SEARCH

## THE BIG IDEA
God loves to rescue lost sinners, and bring them to his feast in his kingdom. Our part is to accept the invitation and walk home, even when discipleship is costly.

## SUMMARY
This study focuses on three scenes and the parables Jesus tells in each. First, Jesus is at a Pharisee's house, and Jesus' teaching springs from the statement that "blessed is the one who will eat at the feast in the kingdom of God" (14 v 15). Jesus presses on his hearers their urgent need to be humble about their standing before God, which overflows into their treatment of others (v 7-14); and their urgent need to respond properly to their invitation to the kingdom (v 15-24).

Second, Jesus is addressing large crowds following him (14 v 25). To them, he underlines the radical cost of true

discipleship, and encourages them not to begin what they have not costed and committed to finish (v 26-35).

Third, Jesus uses three parables to explain why he welcomes tax collectors and sinners (15 v 1), in answer to the muttering of the self-righteous religious leaders (v 2). Motivated by love, Jesus has come to search and find those who are lost. As a shepherd searches for a lost sheep (v 3-7), and a woman hunts for her lost coin (v 8-10), and a father runs to his errant son (v 11-32), so Jesus is the divine rescue mission. Those who know they are lost respond with joy, as does God when a sinner repents; those who think they don't need rescuing respond with pride and anger (v 28-30).

## OPTIONAL EXTRA
Ask your group each to bring some of their

favorite food. Assign some to bring savory and some sweet. Enjoy a "banquet" of eclectic tastes before you begin studying Jesus' words at the Pharisee's meal about the banquet in heaven.

## GUIDANCE FOR QUESTIONS

**1. Have you ever rejected an invitation or offer that you later wished you'd accepted?**

- **Have you ever ducked a difficult challenge that you later realized you should have taken on?**

Have your own answer to both these questions prepared ahead of time. Your group will likely have a range of answers, from funny to more serious.

You could link back to this question after Q7 and/or Q12. God's call to us—and through us to those around us—is both a wonderful invitation to enjoy life with him eternally, and a difficult challenge because it involves loyalty to Jesus and carrying our own cross.

**2. What statement does someone eating with Jesus make (v 15)?** "Blessed is the one who will eat at the feast in the kingdom of God." Ask your group to put this in their own words. The most truly happy and fulfilled person is the person who is confident that they will enjoy the riches of God's presence, under his King, forever.

**3. Who misses out on that banquet?**

- **v 7-11:** Those who seek to exalt themselves and to push themselves forward, either in men's sight or in God's. Jesus envisions a party where a very important person shows up after the guests have been seated. At that point, the host would have to find a place of honor for him, as it would be a tremendous breach of etiquette not to give him an appropriate seat. Realistically,

the host would not be willing to ask everyone at the table to shift down a spot; that would result in chaos. Instead, he will choose one person to relocate from the center of the party all the way down to the last open seat.

Likewise, someone who seeks to claim glory from others or God will find that God is a God who humbles the proud.

- **v 16-20 (Think about what kind of real-life people the characters in the parable would represent.):** People who are too busy with life or too in love with the things of this life to begin or continue the life of discipleship:
  - v 18 is a financial excuse: and many are so busy seeking to make money or acquire a certain standard of living that they reject the invitation to God's kingdom.
  - v 19 is an occupational excuse: and many are so busy seeking promotion or chasing a career that they reject the invitation to God's kingdom.
  - v 20 is a familial excuse: and many are so unwilling to risk a relationship or to rock the boat with their family or friends that they reject the invitation to God's kingdom.

⊻

- **How does the host respond to those excuses (v 21, 24)?** With anger towards those who responded so rudely to the invitation, and with determination that his banquet will nonetheless be full. Those who said they did not want to come would get exactly what they chose (v 24)—to their eternal regret.

**4. Who *is* included in the banquet (v 11, 21-23)?** Those who are humble, and do not seek to push themselves forward or take glory and honor (v 11). The opportunity to feast is now extended to the less desirable members of society: those who cannot lend any prestige to the gathering and whose only qualification for attendance is their willingness to accept the invitation. Those who think they have something better to do miss out; those who know they do not, get in.

**5. What is the path to the banquet at Jesus' eternal table like (v 26-27)?** Very, very hard:

- v 26: We are to love Jesus so much that we "hate" all else by comparison, including our closest family members. (It is best to take Jesus' words in verse 26 in terms of priority—Jesus must have our absolute loyalty and commitment. This was a Hebraic way of speaking, to highlight the need to make something an absolute priority, even over another important claim.)

- v 27: We must carry our cross in order to follow Jesus (see 9 v 23). In Jesus' day, a cross was not a piece of jewelry or a symbol of love and devotion. It was a repulsive means of execution, a way of terrorizing a population and putting down dissent. The crowds in Jesus' day would have seen condemned people carrying the horizontal piece of a cross out to the place of their execution. The call to carry one's cross is a call to a one-way trip to death. That is the level of commitment that following Jesus requires.

**6. Jesus was being followed by "large crowds" (v 25). Why do you think he chose to tell them the mini-parables of verses 28-32? (Hint: Verse 33 is helpful!)** Jesus' point in the parables is: *Don't start without considering the cost and committing to finishing, despite that cost.*

The tower-builder needs not just to begin, but to finish. The king needs to work out whether the price he would pay in battle against greater numbers is outweighed by the victory he may gain. Jesus does not want to be followed by "large crowds" of half-committed followers. He is only interested in fully committed, cross-carrying disciples. So Jesus makes it clear that being his disciple will cost a person everything that they have (v 33). The cost of discipleship is particular to each individual. Jesus requires every person to renounce one hundred percent of what they have, whether that be very little or very much.

**7. APPLY: Think about how you talk about the Christian life to others. How is that similar or different than Jesus' description here?**
- **If there are differences, why? And what effect does that have on people's Christian lives?**

Ask your group to think both about how they speak to other Christians, and to those investigating Christianity.

It is easy for us pay lip service to the call to discipleship without actually sacrificing to follow Christ. We can easily confirm in others the view that being a disciple should not be too hard, or particularly costly. We can find ourselves counseling each other to be "sensible" instead of sacrificial. But when Jesus puts us in a position where we must take up our cross or turn back from him, this kind of attitude will cause us to back out of the Christian life. We need to challenge it in each other, not be compromised by it or encourage it.

Jesus' call to radical discipleship also means that when we proclaim the gospel to unbelievers, we must tell them that following Jesus means that he has a claim to everything in their lives; nothing is off-limits to or outside of his lordship. If they are not told about the cost of discipleship, they may well begin down that path like the man building a tower or the king going to war, only to discover midway through that they do not have what it takes to finish the undertaking.

**8. How do these two parables explain why Jesus is welcoming and eating with "sinners" (15 v 1-2)?** The muttering disapproval of the religious leaders (v 2) seemed to be based on the fact that Jesus was actively cultivating fellowship with "tax collectors and sinners" ( v 1); he was actually welcoming and eating with them.

But Jesus is like the shepherd who, rather than writing off the lost sheep (after all, he has 99 others), is determined to find and bring back that sheep; and like the woman who values the coin and is determined to work hard to find it. And Jesus is also like the shepherd and woman in his joy over finding what was lost. This is why he is actively seeking those who are lost in their own rebellion—because he loves them, and he seeks the joy of restoring them.

**9. What did it take to rescue the sheep and find the coin?** Great effort. The risks of heading out to look for a stray sheep would have been huge for a shepherd. The terrain was treacherous and dangerous. These were not English fields, but Middle Eastern hills. Likewise, locating a coin in the dark on an uneven earth floor would not be a simple task, and carried no guarantee of success. The point is that both the shepherd and the woman chose the harder path in order to find what was lost, such was their commitment.

- **What did the lost sheep and the lost coin contribute to the rescue?** Nothing, other than the sheep wandering off in the

first place.

**10. How is the younger son like the sheep and the coin?**
- He wanders off, in his case deliberately, into treacherous territory.
- He requires a rescue or a "finding" in order to be restored.
- He is brought home (by his father) and the homecoming causes great rejoicing.

- **How is the older son a warning to the Pharisees who were muttering back in verse 2?** The contrast between the two sons could not be starker: while the one left the family to squander his money in shameful ways, the other stayed and served his father obediently (v 29). When he finds out the reason for the celebration going on in the house (v 26-27), he can barely be civil. His bitterness pours out as he describes his time working for his father as slavery (v 29), and as he tries to pour cold water on the father's joy by reminding him that "your son" (not "my brother"!) squandered the family fortune on prostitutes (v 30). And he ends up outside the party.

It is clear that the older brother is meant to show the Pharisees how their muttering about Jesus' ministry places them outside of God's program of restoration and forgiveness. Their complaints are the older brother's complaints. And it will lead them to become estranged from the God they claim to serve. In the end, Jesus is confronting the religious leaders with their failure to understand what brings joy to God. They believe that God delights in those people who, like themselves, seem righteous. The irony is that the people who are most truly lost are those who identify themselves with the 99 "good" sheep who do not need to be found.

## EXPLORE MORE

**Read Ezekiel 34 v 2-6 ... What are they [the leaders of Israel—the shepherds] not doing?** They are not taking care of the flock—particularly not the "weak ... sick or ... injured." They have not "searched for the lost." Instead, they have used God's people for their own ends.

**Read Ezekiel 34 v 11-13. What did God promise would happen, and who would achieve this?** His lost sheep would be found and looked after in their own good pasture. God himself would do this.

**How have we seen Jesus fulfilling that promise in Luke 15?** He is the good shepherd who pursues the sheep. He does what the older brother in the parable should have done; he pursues the lost children of his Father.

**11. APPLY: In what way is it easy for committed Christians to become muttering Pharisees?** It is easy for us to think that our obedience to God means that we (and only we) should be rewarded by God, or more rewarded by God. If we grow irritated that others who do not obey as we do are blessed by God, or if we end up feeling that someone who has sinned grievously against God should not be allowed to enjoy salvation, then we are like the Pharisees here. **Why is that dangerous?** Because it leads us to grow angry with God and refuse his invitation to us to be saved by his grace, on the basis of his love.

**12. APPLY: How is this insight into what brings heaven joy both a thrill for us and a challenge to us?** As sinners, we need to remember that if we have turned to Christ, God delights in us. He takes joy in our return to him, not because we are holy and good but because we are his rescued people. It is thrilling to know that heaven is overjoyed by repentance—and that God delights to love us because he loves us, not because we are good.

But as sinners, we are also challenged to remember that our self-righteous goodness is not what merits us salvation or causes God joy; and to look on others with the same compassion as God does.

---

# 3 Luke 16 v 1 – 18 v 8
# THE KINGDOM IS COMING

## THE BIG IDEA

The King has come, but we are waiting for his kingdom to arrive in all its glorious fullness. That coming kingdom should shape all our thoughts, priorities and actions until it comes.

## SUMMARY

Again, the focus here is on how the reality of the coming King, bringing judgment and salvation as he brings his kingdom in all its fullness, should affect the priorities and lives of the King's subjects in every way.

The focus in chapter 16 is on wealth. We are to make spending decisions in light of eternity (16 v 1-12); we are to beware serving money, for it will prevent us from serving God (v 13-15); and we are to remember that wealth cannot buy us out of hell (v 19-31).

17 v 1 – 18 v 8 centers on the promise and warning of 17 v 20-37—the Son of Man will return in power, and for judgment, and people must be ready. The surrounding sections (see Q10) give various practical details of what it looks like to live with faith in the time between the first and second comings of our King.

## OPTIONAL EXTRA

Jesus' call in 17 v 20-37 is that we be waiting in readiness for an event—his return—whose date we do not know. Have fun with your group competing on a rapid-response task, where they must wait and then react as fast as possible. E.g. humanbenchmark.com/tests/reactiontime

## GUIDANCE FOR QUESTIONS

**1. What stops people becoming Christians, or stops people continuing to live as Christians?** There are an almost infinite number of "right answers," and your group will already have seen some in the responses to Jesus so far in Luke's Gospel. Having taken some ideas from your group, you could tell them that the two that this study highlights, from the passages you will be enjoying, are a love of money, and a lack of remembering that the kingdom will come one day, but has not come yet (a theme introduced by Jesus in chapter 12, and focused on once more here in chapters 17 – 18).

**2. What does the manager do with his position, and why?** Facing the loss of his position, he calls in each of his master's debtors, asks how much they owe, and writes down the debt. His motive is in verse 4: "When I lose my job here, people will welcome me into their houses."

**3. What lesson does Jesus draw for his followers, and why (v 8-9)?** The people who belong to the world and all its values (literally "the sons of this age") know how to get what they want from other people through clever planning and activity. God's children (literally "the sons of light"), however, sometimes fail to see how they can shrewdly use the things of this world to their spiritual advantage. The citizens of the world know how to take care of their needs and make sure they get what they want. The dishonest steward behaves wisely according to the world's standards and the world's values. In an analogous way, Jesus wants his followers to behave wisely according to the standards and values of his kingdom.
So Jesus says his followers should use their wealth to "gain friends for yourselves" (v 9). That is to say, we should live with the kind of generosity that is attractive to others; after all, generous people usually have lots of friends. One of the blessings of these friendships is that when your money fails you, you will be welcomed into eternal dwellings. Who knows how our acts of service, our faithful sharing of the gospel, and our generosity toward others might impact people's lives—and result in a warm welcome when we reach heaven from those we have impacted?

**4. What warnings does Jesus give about our attitude toward money [in v 13-15]?**
- v 13: If our hearts are committed to money as our master, they cannot be committed to God. The miser, the workaholic, the over-spender, and the person who spends a great portion of their time worrying about their finances each lives in service to money as their god.
- v 14: Notice that the Pharisees—those who were religious and respected—were also lovers of money.

- v 15: God "knows your hearts"—we can pay lip service to generosity to the things of God, but he knows perfectly well whether we actually love him or our money.

## EXPLORE MORE
### In what way have things been different since the time of John the Baptist? The
Law and the Prophets were proclaimed; but now, "the good news of the kingdom of God is being preached." The arrival of the Messiah represented the beginning of that new era, and so the old way of doing things was defunct. Now the good news of the kingdom is being preached and the promise of the Law and Prophets has been fulfilled. We no longer relate to God as Old Testament believers did, through faith in an as-yet-unfulfilled promise, but we relate to him based on faith in what he did for us through the death and resurrection of his Son. Now the "narrow door" is open to those who are willing to make the effort to walk through it (v 16, see 13 v 24).

### In what sense are they the same (v 17—see also Matthew 5 v 17-18)?
Even though the Old Testament has been supplanted by the proclamation of the good news of the kingdom, "the least stroke of a pen" can never "drop out of the Law". Instead, Jesus understood that his arrival signified the fulfillment of the Law (see Matthew 5 v 17-18). Far from nullifying the Law, Jesus was bringing it to its ultimate purpose. He was fulfilling the promise and meaning of the Old Testament in his life, his teaching, and his substitutionary death and resurrection.

### What does Jesus say his followers are to do when it comes to divorce (v 18)?
They should not pursue divorce in order to marry someone else. The general principle is

clear: re-marriage after a divorce is normally forbidden (depending on the make-up of your group, you may want to pause here to read Matthew 19 v 9 and 1 Corinthians 7 v 15, pointing out that unfaithfulness and abandonment are permissible cases for divorce)

### Read Deuteronomy 24 v 1-4 and Genesis 2 v 18-25. Is Jesus' standard higher or lower than that of "the Law and the Prophets"? What does this tell us about Jesus' approach to the law? Jesus' words
here represent a more rigorous ethical standard than that which is contained in the Old Testament. The law contained regulations for how divorce should be handled so that the woman, who was the more vulnerable party in the proceedings, would not be destroyed in the process. But here Jesus presses on his followers the expectation that they will seek to go beyond the law and comply with God's original intent for marriage.

### 5. In what sense is this parable [in 16 v 19-31] a warning to those who are wealthy? The first—unnamed—man we are
introduced to was rich. He enjoyed all the luxuries that worldly wealth could provide (v 19). The rich man was clearly aware of the beggar Lazarus' presence at his gate and his extreme need, for he knew the beggar's name without being told (v 24). But there is no indication that he ever did anything to address the poor man's longing and suffering, even though the Old Testament demanded such from him (Deuteronomy 15 v 7-8); the rich man never points to any act of kindness on his part that might mitigate his guilt.

The rich man, however, goes to Hades (the realm of the dead), where he is in torment (v 23) and agony (v 25). Notice that his life of wealth and power had conditioned him to being in charge, and so in his pride he attempts to boss people around, even in Hades! But in death he finds himself quite alone, with a chasm fixed between heaven and hell that prevents Lazarus from traveling between the two places, even if Abraham were inclined to send him (v 26).

Wealth will not bring us to heaven. And wealth often produces a pride that brings us to hell.

- **In what sense is it a warning to those who have access to clear Bible teaching?** The formerly rich man asks for a word of warning to be extended toward his five brothers so that they might avoid his fate (v 27-28). Abraham's response (v 29) presses home the sufficiency and importance of God's word. The five brothers do not need a special visitor, for they have already received a supernatural revelation of God's will—Moses and the Prophets. If they will not listen to them, then they will not listen even to a man who comes to them from beyond the dead (v 31). We are not lacking in access to God's revelation and the truths it contains. We can only be lacking in our willingness to listen and respond to it.

- **So how is it a challenge to "the Pharisees, who loved money" (v 14)?** Here are a group with access to the Scriptures but who will not listen to them, and who are in love with wealth, which causes them to proudly sneer (v 14). Both the rich man and his brothers can be seen to be a warning to them.

### 6. APPLY: In what ways do you as a church find it easy to excuse loving and serving money as your real Master?

The answer to this will vary according to your context. But if your church is in the West, there ought to be some challenging answers, since materialism is one of the most popular gods of a consumerist society, and the gods of our culture are the gods we most easily adopt and excuse without noticing. If you are in an affluent area, the questions may be: What living standards do you assume you should have? What salaries do you justify making sacrifices to achieve? If you are in a poorer area, what are the lifestyles that are being chased? Is there a sense that money, if only you had it, would solve various problems?

- **What would someone who is "kingdom-shrewd" with their wealth look like in your context?** Kingdom shrewdness is what Jesus describes in verse 9—we use our worldly wealth now in a way that shows we care more about our eternal future than our current situation. Use your answers to the first part of the question to think about what would be different if eternity was the driving factor in how you view and use the money you have. The answers will likely be very challenging!

### 7. In what sense was the kingdom of God already "in [their] midst" ([17] v 21), do you think?

Jesus himself was the embodiment of the kingdom. The kingdom of God, in the person of its King, was standing right in front of them—it had already come!

- **But what does Jesus also tell his disciples (v 22-25)?** In the future they will "long to see one of the days of the Son of Man, but you will not see it" (v 22). This is a reference to Jesus' return to earth in splendor to judge God's enemies and vindicate his people—to put it another way, to establish his kingdom in all its powerful fullness. So though the King has come, the kingdom is not yet fully come—and the disciples will not see it in the short term. But when it does come, it will be dramatic and visible to all (v 24).

**8. So in what sense had the kingdom already arrived, and in what sense had the kingdom not yet arrived?** This question draws together the teaching of v 20-25. The kingdom had arrived in the person of its King, whose life, death, resurrection, and ascension opened his kingdom to anyone who asks for forgiveness from the King. But the kingdom has not yet arrived in all its fullness, which will happen when the King returns in all his power and glory to judge and to save.

**9. What does Jesus say the future coming of the kingdom will be like (v 26-37)?** Because it will come suddenly and decisively (v 28-29, 34-35), people will be caught unaware by the arrival of God's judgment. They will be going about their normal daily lives on the day that the Son of Man is revealed, and they will perish like the people in Noah's day (v 26-27) and in the days of Lot (v 28-29). "It will be just like this on the day the Son of Man is revealed" (v 30). There will be no opportunity to make preparations once that day has arrived (v 31); they must not fail to obey the Lord's instructions as Lot's wife did (v 32—see Genesis 19 v 26). Where she allowed the comforts of home to distract her from the urgency of the Lord's deliverance, we must not be so enamored of the pleasures of our daily routine that we fail to follow Jesus with our whole hearts and lives. In light of that reality, Jesus repeats his call to discipleship in Luke 17 v 33: "Whoever tries to keep their life will lose it, and whoever loses their life will preserve it" (see 9 v 24).

• **What are the dangers of forgetting the time we live in—after the King came, and before the kingdom comes fully?** We will give up on Jesus because he does not deliver what he never promised—the fullness of the kingdom right now. Or we will run after those who claim that he has already come (v 23). Or we will worry that he will never come, or that we may miss his coming.

**10. What principles for living in this "already/not yet" tension do verses 1-19 give us?**
• **v 1-3a:** We still live in a fallen world and so must watch out for temptations to sin, and be very careful not to tempt others to sin.

• **v 3b-4:** Our kingdom commitment to righteousness means that we have an obligation to confront sin in the lives of other believers, particularly when our brother sins against us. Obviously, that confrontation needs to be undertaken with a spirit of love and humility (see Galatians 6 v 1), but merely turning a blind eye to sin is to forget that the King is returning and that his standards matter. Jesus' coming kingdom means we are serious about holiness.
Further, we will need to forgive one another. This can be difficult and painful, but we follow a King who came to forgive us, and we anticipate a kingdom where all will be forgiven, we will live with our brothers and sisters, and justice will be done. So we do not need to get justice now; but we do need to anticipate our future by forgiving now. Jesus' coming kingdom means we forgive.

• **v 5-6:** We need to ask for faith! And we

need to understand how strong the object of our faith is—even small faith in our great Lord is sufficient to keep us going until he returns. Jesus' coming kingdom means we keep asking for faith in him. **Note:** We are not meant to put Jesus' words to the test by trying to relocate shrubbery using nothing but our faith. Those seeking to "prove" their faith through such dramatic signs have more in common with magicians and street charlatans than with the apostles' ministry of preaching, teaching, and healing.

- **v 7-10:** Our obedience is what we owe God—not something that earns us a place in his kingdom, nor allows us to be proud. Our obedience never puts God in our debt. Understanding this means we give glory to God, not to ourselves. Jesus' coming kingdom means we are humble.

- **v 11-19:** Following on from this, we are characterized by gratitude, just as the healed lepers should have been. The surprise of this story is that only one ex-leper returned to say thank you. This man alone had faith, and so this man alone was healed spiritually (v 19—the Greek word used there is literally "saved"). Jesus' coming kingdom means we are grateful.

- **18 v 1-8:** Jesus makes the point of this parable clear in verse 1: we are to pray, and not give up. In context, it is not about persistence in prayer generally (though that is a good thing), but prayer regarding the return of Jesus: so that when he returns he will find his people praying for that return, and for the justice it will bring. Jesus' coming kingdom means we are prayerful about that day.

**11. APPLY: What reasons for failing to start loving, or keep loving, God do**

these chapters of Luke offer us?
- Love of money
- Lack of understanding of, or confidence in, the past coming of the kingdom in the person of King Jesus; and the future, full arrival of that kingdom upon his return.

- **How do they also offer us the solutions to these reasons?** Let your group recap the warnings Jesus gave about the love of money, and where it leads, and how to live "kingdom-shrewdly" instead; and the assurances and details of his return that he gave. Notice also verse 25—Jesus not only predicted his return (which had not happened as he spoke, and still has not) but also his suffering and rejection (which had not happened as he spoke, but which did transpire and which should give us confidence that he knows what will come to pass).

# 4 Luke 18 v 9 – 19 v 44
# INS AND OUTS

## THE BIG IDEA

We come into Jesus' kingdom by coming to him as our King with empty hands, confessing our sin and asking for his mercy. We live in Jesus' kingdom by following him wholeheartedly and using all he gives us in his service.

## SUMMARY

The parable at the start of this section (18 v 9-14) is meant to answer the question: *who is truly part of God's kingdom?* In answering, Jesus destroys the fundamental principle of pretty much every religion! The good, law-abiding, morally upstanding Pharisee is not justified (v 14). But the tax collector, a self-confessed sinner, is— because he is humble enough to ask for mercy rather than holding up his goodness. There follows a series of interactions between Jesus and various individuals/ groups. Each reflect the parable in reality:

- The children are like the tax collector, coming to Jesus but not offering anything to Jesus (v 15-17).
- The rich young ruler comes as the Pharisee did, confident in his law-keeping but unwilling to make Jesus his absolute priority in life, and so goes away sad (v 18-29).
- The blind beggar is like the tax collector, asking Jesus for help (v 35-42).
- The tax collector, Zacchaeus, is like the tax collector (19 v 1-10)!

The end of this section sees Jesus enter Jerusalem—the end of the journey he began back in 9 v 51. The parable of 19 v 11-27 tells of the arrival of a king who is rejected, a picture of what will happen in Jerusalem.

But it also encourages the King's servants to use their time and gifts wisely, so that they might look forward to hearing those wonderful words when the King returns: "Well done, my good servant!" (v 17).

## OPTIONAL EXTRA

Collect many objects of different sizes and shapes. Challenge each member of your group to pick up as many as they can at the same time. Let the "champion" have one more go—and then offer them a large cake / bottle of wine / something else desirable, if they can hold it as well. Of course, they'll find it impossible (hopefully!) The point is that if we fill our hands with things, we are in no position to receive something better. And when we approach God with our "hands full" of our goodness, or cling onto what this world says we need, then we are unable simply to receive his mercy and gift of eternal life—as Jesus' interactions with people in this passage show.

## GUIDANCE FOR QUESTIONS

**1. What is necessary for someone to enter God's eternal kingdom?** The obvious "Christian" answer is "faith." We are so familiar with phrases like "Put your faith in Jesus" or "Repent and believe" that oftentimes we don't stop to ask what that actually means, and what that actually looks like. Encourage your group to add detail to their answer if they simply say "faith." You could also ask your group to think of how people shopping in their local mall would answer.

- **What prevents people from entering his kingdom?** There are no "wrong" answers to this. You could return to it as you look at the Pharisee in Jesus' parable of 18 v 9-14 (Q3) and the rich young ruler (Q4).

**2. What is good about the Pharisee (v 10-12)?** The Pharisees were widely respected for their piety and devotion to the Torah, and this particular man's religious rigor (as described in verse 12, and we have no reason to doubt his truthfulness) exceeded that which God required of his people in the Law of Moses. The Pharisee is living a more obedient live than other people (v 11).

- **How does his prayer reveal his society's attitudes toward tax collectors?** He lists the tax collector alongside "robbers, evildoers, adulterers" (v 12)—as those whom it is good not to be like. Jesus assumes his listeners will not be surprised by this association. Tax collectors, because they worked for the occupying Romans and grew rich through over-taxing the people, were widely despised as traitors, thieves, and oppressors of their own people.

**3. Why is Jesus' verdict in verse 14 shocking?** The traitorous thief is "justified"—right with God, with no charge against him. And the "other"—the Pharisee—is not. It is hard to overstate how shocking and revolutionary Jesus' conclusion is: the justified one is the sinner who approaches God on the basis of his mercy, rather than the "good" man who approaches God on his own merit. Jesus is destroying the fundamental principles of pretty much every religion!

- **How does it answer the question: who is part of God's kingdom?** This question reinforces what you have already seen—

the sinful person who accepts they are sinful and comes to God asking for mercy receives it. The person who is less sinful, but comes to God assuming his approval on the basis of their goodness, does not receive mercy and so is not a member of God's kingdom.

**4. How do we see the themes of that parable [in 18 v 9-14] in the approach of each person/group to Jesus; and in the relationship with Jesus they finish the episode with?**

- **18 v 15-17:** Western societies today tend to idealize children as innocent—this was unknown in Jesus' day. Children were down with tax collectors in terms of people with whom an important rabbi would never think to concern himself. The disciples' actions here would be perfectly justified in most people's eyes. But Jesus welcomes the children—because the quality they possess is their unworthiness (they have no résumé of spiritual accomplishments to lay out before Jesus). They approach him in the same way the tax collector did. It is this kind of person, who simply comes pleading no goodness, who enters the kingdom (and only this kind of person, v 16). The children end up hearing Jesus' welcome of them.
  **Note:** The danger here is that we interpret Jesus' words too romantically. He is not saying that children are so innocent and lovely that they are worthy of the kingdom of God (or, as some have understood this passage, that they should be baptized); quite the opposite.

- **18 v 18-25:** If the children remind us of the tax collector's unworthiness, this ruler reminds us of the Pharisee in the temple. He had a lot going for him, spiritually speaking. He was wealthy (v 23), which both would have enabled him to give alms generously (see v 12) and also would have been interpreted as a sign of God's favor (hence the disciples' astonishment in verse 26). He was also a keeper of the law from his youth (v 20-21), a claim that Jesus does not bother to dispute.

But he ends up very sad (v 23), and (as Mark 10 v 22 makes clear) walks away from Jesus and from eternal life. Jesus has lasered in on the thing that the man loves very much—more in fact than he loves God: his wealth. He wants the kingdom on his own terms. He is not prepared to give up everything else in order to have it. Don't miss the force of Jesus' words in Luke 18 v 24-25—the more possessions we have, the greater their gravitational pull on our hearts. For the wealthy, the narrow door of 13 v 24 has now been reduced to the width of the eye of a needle (18 v 25).

- **18 v 35-43:** Here is a real man—a beggar—asking Jesus for what Jesus' fictional tax collector had asked God for—mercy. He brings a determination to cry out to Jesus that will not be silenced by those around him. He knows that Jesus has both the ability and the willingness to give him mercy. And he uses his new-found sight to follow Jesus, praising God (v 43).

- **19 v 1-10:** Zacchaeus is a real tax collector! He was a wildly successful thief (v 2) and a traitor to his people; this was the kind of "sinner" (v 7) that seemed to be obviously outside of God's program of salvation. But he responds to Jesus inviting himself into Zacchaeus' house (and life) by welcoming him gladly (v 6). He does what the other rich man in these episodes, back in 18 v 18-25, would not—he gives his wealth away (19 v 8). He has found real salvation in welcoming the Son of Man into his life (v 9-10).

If your group have not already mentioned it, point out that the blind beggar and Zacchaeus show us that membership of the kingdom is transformative. Receiving the love of Jesus has a profound impact on people's lives. Before his healing, the blind man probably desperately wanted to see so that he could live a "normal" life. But once Jesus healed him, he did not use his new gift to go back home and make himself comfortable. Instead, he went to see the world as one of Jesus' followers. Before Jesus befriended him, Zacchaeus' life was committed to the pursuit of ill-gotten wealth. But once Jesus came into his life, he was transformed into a man who could joyfully give away half of his goods to those in need and make restitution to those he had wronged.

### EXPLORE MORE

**Jesus' final words in these episodes reveal that his mission is "to seek and save the lost" (v 10). Who are the "lost" in these passages?** Everyone! Some are more obviously lost—the tax collector in the parable, the blind beggar, Zacchaeus (despite his wealth). But the children are lost too. And so are the good Pharisee and the rich young ruler. The only real difference between those two groups of people is that the former can see their need for Jesus clearly and the latter is blinded by their own self-righteousness. Both kinds of people need Jesus, but only one kind of person is screaming by the side of the road and climbing up into a tree to get him.

**Read Ezekiel 34 v 11-12, 16. How does Luke show us Jesus fulfilling this promise in real people's real lives?** Luke 19 v 10: Jesus defines his mission as seeking and saving the lost—just as God promised he would come to find his scattered sheep and gather them to him.

Jesus brought salvation to Zacchaeus' house (v 9) as a fulfilment of that promise.

**5. How does 18 v 27-33 answer the following questions:**
• **"Who then can be saved?" (v 26):** The answer is that it is impossible, unless God does it (v 27). The answer to the puzzle of this chapter is there in verses 31-33. Jesus will fulfill "everything that is written by the prophets about the Son of Man" (v 31), particularly with respect to his suffering, death, and resurrection (v 32-33). That is how people with no righteousness of their own can be saved; not through their good works, but by virtue of Jesus' death in their place. On the cross, he took the guilt and shame and weakness of his people, so that when they cry out to God for mercy like the tax collector, they receive forgiveness and righteousness as a free gift (see 2 Corinthians 5 v 21). It is no accident that Luke records this prediction of Jesus' death here, in the midst of all these interactions with different people.

• **Is it worth leaving everything to follow Jesus?** The encounter with the rich ruler reminds us that in order to come into the kingdom, we must renounce our love for and loyalty to everything else. He was promised treasure in heaven but would not part with the treasures of the earth in order to gain them.

But don't miss the surprising conclusion to this conversation in v 29-30. We might expect that the Lord would offer his followers a choice between a good life now (the life that the ruler wanted so badly that he would not part with his wealth) and a good life in eternity. And in fact, following Jesus will mean sacrifice and difficulty in this life (v 28-29; see 6 v 22; 9 v 23-24). But Jesus says that not only will the one who makes sacrifices

for the kingdom of God receive a reward in eternity, but that he or she will also "receive many times as much *in this age*" (18 v 30; italics mine). The Christian life is often difficult, but the gifts that we experience in the present (freedom from slavery to sin, membership in the family of God, fellowship with the people of God) far outweigh the benefits enjoyed by those who cling to their possessions and rebellion against God.

**6. APPLY: What would the attitudes and decisions of the children, the blind beggar and Zacchaeus look like in your own life?**
• **What would the attitude and decisions of the rich young ruler look like in your own life?**
These questions aim to help your group think about how the various "characters" in these parables/interactions would be thinking and living in the very different context that you live in. It is not a case of answering, "The first group would go to church, and the second would not." Pharisees were very, very committed to obedience and to religious practices. Challenge your group to think about what it looks like if you live as a rich young ruler who goes to church each week.

**7. APPLY: What are the danger signs that someone is approaching Jesus like the Pharisee in the parable, rather than the tax collector?** Christians are not immune to the Pharisee's mindset. Whenever we create our own extra-biblical rules and judge other Christians who do not follow them, we are acting like a Pharisee. Whenever we feel that God does not love us because we have sinned or failed, we have adopted the Pharisee's approach. Whenever we are proud of our own goodness, we are acting just like the Pharisee.

Any time we forget that we are sinners in ongoing need of God's mercy, or that we are those to whom God's mercy is given, we will be thrown back onto our "works-righteousness" (which will produce pride, anxiety, or despair).

**8. How does the parable about the nobleman and his subjects warn those who are not submitting to Jesus as King?** Opposing him will have awful consequences. Jesus is going to go away, and when he returns 19 v 27 will become a reality on earth. This is not a popular message—but it is a central part of the gospel.

**9. How does the parable about the nobleman and his servants encourage and warn those who are submitting to him?** Rehearse the story with your group: the nobleman gives a mina each (roughly three months' wages) to ten servants, to "put to work" while he is gone (v 13). Each has to give an account when he gets back (v 15). The story focuses on three of those servants. The first has earned an eleven-fold return on his investment (v 16); the second, six-fold (v 18). The third has done nothing with his mina, other than wrapping it up (v 20). He then chooses to defend himself by insulting his master (v 21—nothing in the parable indicates that the nobleman deserved this characterization; v 17 and 19 show that he is remarkably generous). The first two are rewarded lavishly, being given entire cities to "take charge of" (v 17, 19). The third loses even the mina he had (v 24).

*The encouragement:* Every aspect of a Christian's life is a gift given to them for the purpose of investment for Christ. It is a privilege to be given means with which to serve him. It is remarkable that he promises to richly reward us for our service to him. And it is wonderful to think that, in respect of those areas of our lives where we have invested what we have in his service and for his glory, God will say, "Well done, my good servant!"

*The warning:* One day, God will ask us to give an account for how we used all that he gave us. We are not free to use those things for our own purposes or to neglect them all together.

**10. Read Zechariah 9 v 9-10. What is Jesus claiming:**
• **about who he is?** He is the mighty King promised through the Old Testament. His rule will extend throughout the world. He will be victorious, and his enemies will not be able to stand against him.

• **about what he is like?** He is both "righteous and victorious" but also "lowly." We misunderstand Jesus if we forget his power and majesty or if we forget his humility and servant-heartedness.

• **about what he will do?** He will "proclaim peace" by defeating his enemies and fighting for his people.

**11. How do those present respond to his claims?** The disciples threw their cloaks on the animal and "put Jesus on it" like a king on his throne (Luke 19 v 35).

The people threw their cloaks on the ground in front of him (v 36), a first-century version of rolling out a red carpet.

Some of the Pharisees called on Jesus to rebuke his followers (v 39). They were clearly offended by the claim referenced by the donkey-riding: that Jesus is the promised King.

• **How does Jesus reveal the importance of the choice of how we respond** (v 41-44)? In verse 41, Jesus finally sees Jerusalem, marking the end of a journey that began back in 9 v 51. And he weeps because he knows that Jerusalem will reject him and the peace he offers (v 41-42). They will make themselves his enemies and face the defeat which that brings. Jesus predicts the destruction of the city in graphic terms (v 43-44). He is not delighted about this (he weeps over it); he highlights that the choice to reject him as King will bring terrible judgment.

**12. APPLY: If we look at the world around us in the way Jesus looked at Jerusalem in verses 41-44, what would we...**

• **feel?** We would weep for those who persistently reject the kingship of Jesus. We would not be complacent about their fate, nor would we ever be pleased about that fate.

• **say?** We would speak about the King. We would speak to them of the peace that Jesus is offering, and we would warn them honestly and with tears in our eyes of the alternative to that peace.

• **Does this describe the way you look at those around you who do not submit to Jesus as King? Why / why not?** For many of us, the answer will be "no." There may be many reasons, but none of them are justified. And that should deeply challenge us, for if we follow Jesus, we must surely love the things that he loves, and care about the things that he cares about—and if we do, then we will have the same response to people who persist in rejecting him as he did to Jerusalem.

# 5 Luke 19 v 45 – 21 v 38
# SHOWDOWN AT THE TEMPLE

## THE BIG IDEA
As we wait and long for Jesus' return, we must give God all we have and are, and not use our intellect to find loopholes in Jesus' authority over us, or use our faith to serve ourselves and our agendas.

## SUMMARY
Jesus has now entered the city that kills the prophets (13 v 33-34). The next two chapters take place at the Passover season in the temple complex, where Jesus will teach daily until he is arrested. As it was the center of the Jewish religious life of which Jesus was so critical, it is fitting that the final climactic showdowns of his earthly ministry should take place here at the temple.

This study focuses on the interactions between Jesus and his opponents in which Jesus shows up the duplicity and hypocrisy of his opponents, as well as warning them that, since they are about to kill him, they are about to face God's judgment (20 v 9-19). Those interactions are bookended by Jesus' clearing of the temple and his praise of the widow who gives all she has, which indicate his complete rejection of what Israel's religion has become—a rejection that is picked up on in the difficult section of 21 v 5-36. Here, Jesus is looking forward both to the Roman destruction of Jerusalem (and its temple) in AD 70 *and* to his return. Q9-11 will help your group grapple with this section, and apply it to themselves living in the 21st century, while giving scope for legitimate disagreement on some of the trickier details of the passage.

## OPTIONAL EXTRA

To introduce the adversarial nature of Jesus' teaching and debates with his opponents during these days at the temple, set up a series of fun "showdowns"—e.g. thumb wars, rock-paper-scissors, conducting a dialog where both members must speak using only questions, a staring contest, etc.

## GUIDANCE FOR QUESTIONS

**1. Does intelligence, success or education help or hinder us in our efforts to understand the Bible, do you think? Why?** In this study, we will see the elites of Jerusalem using all their intellect and power to resist Jesus and the truth of his claims; reading the Bible in a way that seeks to support their own prejudices and pride. We will also see a poor widow responding rightly to Scripture, and pleasing God by doing so. Let your group discuss this question openly, without seeking to move them to too firm a conclusion. Of course, learning to read enables us to read our Bibles, and this is a good thing. Learning critical thinking enables us to evaluate different views of a text for ourselves, which is also good. But cleverness itself is not a virtue as such—it can just as easily be used in the service of resisting God as worshiping him.

**2. What is the aim of the chief priests, teachers of the law, and people's leaders (19 v 47)?** "To kill" Jesus. **What is their problem (v 48)?** The people "hung on his words" (v 48)—the only thing keeping the leaders from killing Jesus was

the adoration of the crowds.

**3. What is their first question (20 v 2)? Why is it a clever one to ask?** On what authority was Jesus "doing these things"? Jesus was wildly popular, but he did not have a title or position. Jesus was outside of the religious and political establishment, and so in one sense had no credentials or pedigree to justify his cleansing of the temple (19 v 45-46) and ministry of teaching and healing.

- **What is even cleverer about Jesus' answer in verses 3-4 (v 5-6 will help)?** Jesus' indirect answer concerns John's authority to baptize—was it from heaven or from humans? This forces the leaders into answering their own question, because John had testified that Jesus was the Messiah (3 v 15-18). So the leaders will not want to say John's baptism is from heaven (20 v 5). But John was so beloved by the people that they are terrified of saying that John was not sent by heaven (v 6). And so they wind up weakly refusing to answer (v 7).

- **The leaders had been trying to show up the weakness of Jesus' position, but how does Jesus wind up showing the weakness of theirs?** Their discussion and answer reveal that the truth was far less important to them than the political ramifications of the truth. They—not Jesus—are revealed as the ones who are woefully inadequate to exercise leadership over God's people. They care more about their own position than the truth.

**4. What is their second question (v 22)? Why is it a clever one to ask?** Should the Jewish people pay taxes to the Roman emperor, or not? Again, the goal is to force Jesus to take a position that traps him. If, on one hand, Jesus says that people should not pay the tax, then the scribes and priests can report him to the Romans, who will not hesitate to eliminate anyone who might seem like a threat to the peace of the empire. But if he says that they should pay the tax, then he might be seen as a traitor to the people of Israel and lose the approval of the people, which is the only thing keeping the leaders from arresting Jesus.

- **What is even cleverer about Jesus' answer (v 24-25)?** His response manages both to answer the question and to avoid the trap. In one sense, he affirms the authority of Caesar—since the image on the coin used to pay the tax is Caesar's, it is appropriate to use such a coin to pay such a tax. But at the same time, he limits Caesar's authority—since people are made in God's image, it is right to use our lives to worship God alone. The coin is the extent of the honor that Caesar is due; by contrast, God deserves all that humanity has and is.

- **How does Jesus here show us the Christian view of how we relate to authorities?** Followers of Christ should be law-abiding citizens wherever they live (unless obeying the law of man would require someone to disobey God—see Acts 5 v 29), and that includes paying taxes. If you have time, turn to Romans 13 v 1-2 and/or 1 Peter 2 v 13-17. But we are not to invest our hopes in human rulers. No Caesar can save us, and we are free from having to give them more than what they are owed—namely, respect and conditional obedience. Since we are made in God's image, only he deserves (and can justly command) our ultimate love and allegiance.

**5. Who asks the third question, and**

what is it **(20 v 27-33)?** The Sadducees, who did not believe in the resurrection of the dead (v 27), ask: if a woman was married to seven brothers in this life(!), who will she be married to in God's eternal kingdom? **Why is it a clever question?** Because it makes the whole idea of resurrection and eternal life seem ridiculous. If we are raised from the dead, how can we possibly untangle all of the things that happen during our lives and after our deaths?

- **How does Jesus answer (v 34-38)?** The critical flaw in the Sadducees' thinking is that they assume life after death is just like life now. But Jesus says marriage is an institution for "this age" alone (v 34)—there will be no marriage in the age to come (v 35—Jesus does not say explicitly why this is; it could be because there is no longer a need to replenish the population through procreation, since people "can no longer die"). So the answer to the question is: none of them!

- **How does Jesus here show us part of the Christian view of marriage?** The marriages that we enjoy here on earth are meant to give us a picture and foretaste of the far greater reality of our union with Christ that we will enjoy in eternity (Ephesians 5 v 31-32; Revelation 19 v 6-9). Human marriage, great though it is, is merely a preview; once the reality has come, it will no longer be necessary, and (strange as this may seem now) it will not be missed.

**EXPLORE MORE**
**Who asks the question that initiates the fourth discussion (20 v 41)?** Jesus.
**What is the answer to the question of verse 44?** The question is: how can the coming Messiah be both David's son and

also his "Lord"? That is, why does the great King David call this descendant of his his "Lord" (in a society where children spoke to their fathers with formal respect, but fathers would never do so to their children). The only possible answer is that the Messiah must be both in David's family line and also God's Son (and thus David's Lord). Though the conclusion is left unstated, the point is obvious: Jesus is the only one who makes sense of all the data—he is God's Son, born into David's line.

**6. How does Jesus' parable in verses 9-16 provide his assessment of what is really going on?** The vineyard was an image used in the OT to represent the nation of Israel (e.g. Isaiah 5 v 1-7; Psalm 80 v 8-18). The tenants of the parable, who refuse to pay the rent of a share of the fruit, are the leaders of Israel. The servants are the prophets, who called on the people of Israel to produce the obedience and justice and worship they owed to the Lord. The leaders' final, terrible act will be to kill the owner's son—Jesus. Jesus is explaining that the leaders' rejection of him will lead to his execution by them—and that this is a rejection of God, whose Son he is, and will lead to the removal from office of those "tenants," the leaders (v 16).

• **What is tragically ironic about the response of the teachers of the law and the chief priests to the parable (v 19)?** Jesus says, *You will show your rejection of God by killing me, his Son*— and the leaders know he is talking about them, and yet respond by looking harder for a way to arrest him. It is tragically ironic that Jesus says, *You are about to kill me,* and they respond by thinking, *We are going to kill him.*

**7. Compare 19 v 45-46 and 20 v 45-47 with 21 v 1-4. What religious approaches does Jesus criticize, and what religious approach does he praise?** *Jesus criticizes:* (1) The use of religion for personal gain (19 v 45-46), and pursuing a form of godly religion (then in the temple, now in Christianity) that prevents people coming into a forgiven relationship with God. (The quote in v 46 comes from Isaiah 56 v 7, where God is seeing a day when all peoples, both Jews and Gentiles, will come to pray to him in his temple in Jerusalem.) (2) The use of religion to further one's personal glory and honor (20 v 45-46), and which uses others, particularly the weak and vulnerable, to further that end.
*Jesus praises:* The poor widow: her two copper coins (21 v 1-5) seem like an insignificant offering, especially compared to the greater gifts being offered. But Jesus praises her for giving all she has. She is dedicating all she has to the God in whose image she is made.

**8. APPLY: Sum up what you have learned about:**
• **the life of true discipleship that pleases Jesus.** Think about how you can, in your circumstances and given what the Lord has chosen to give each of you, live in the same way as that poor widow. What would it look like for you to "give … to God what is God's" (20 v 25)?

• **the life of false religion that Jesus opposes.** Consider how the Bible can be misused to resist Jesus' call to radical discipleship or allow ourselves to doubt his authority over us; how we might use our church or faith for our own gain, glory, or honor; how we might indulge our preferences in a way that prevents others coming to hear about or feel welcomed by Jesus, and/or his people.

- **Why is it challenging that Jesus' greatest opponents were the most religious people around him?** Because Christians tend to be serious about knowing the Bible, obeying God's law, seeking to hold positions that allow them to influence their society, and being different than the world around—just as the Pharisees and Sadducees were (or thought they were). However, these things do not insulate us from ending up opposing Jesus' rule and priorities. In fact, they can make it easier to do it, and harder to spot that we are doing it.

**9. Which parts of [21 v 8-36] do you think are describing the events of AD 70 and the fall of Jerusalem, and which the events of Jesus' return, which still lies in the future? Which seem unclear?** Do not spend too long on this question, or get bogged down in details or people's personal opinions (which are sometimes, in this area, very firmly held). The aim of this question is simply to help your group see that it is possible to understand this teaching; but it is necessary to handle it carefully, rather than assuming it all applies to "the end times."

Here is how I think the passage relates to AD 70 and to Jesus' return:

- v 8-24: AD 70 (though of course there are truths here for us to treasure in our day)
- v 25-28: Jesus' return
- v 29-33: Unclear, but likely AD70 (see v 32)
- v 34-36: Both (it is both about "what is about to happen," v 36, and about what will "come on all those who live on the face of the whole earth, v 35)

**10. What does Jesus want his followers to:**
- **watch out for (v 8-9)?** Those who claim

to be the returning Messiah. 21 v 27 indicates that Jesus' return will not be ambiguous.

- **make up their minds about (v 12-19)?** Not to worry about how to respond when rejected, persecuted or facing death. Jesus will be there with them, giving them words, and watching over their souls (which, given v 16, must be what v 18 means).

- **look forward to (v 25-28)?** The Son of Man coming in all his glory and power. We should live with our heads up, longing for the return of Christ.

- **be careful about (v 34)?** To live each day in light of Christ's return—not to allow our hearts to become gripped by the things of this world, the daily temptations and distractions that can easily take root if we take our eyes off Christ's coming return.

- **pray for (v 36)?** That we will keep trusting Christ, so that we are able to "stand before the Son of Man," forgiven, when he returns.

**11. APPLY: Looking through your answers to Question Ten, how can you help each other to do each of these things? What might cause you not to do them?** Think about particular circumstances that might cause you to stop doing these things. What would you need your Christian friends to remind you of or do for you? What would be the most unhelpful things they could say?

# 6 Luke 22 v 1-71
# A NIGHT OF TRIALS

## THE BIG IDEA
Jesus loves the people who fail him, and he stood for the truth when others denied it. We are to seek to stand loyal to him; and when we fail, we are to weep, but also to remember that he did not fail us, so we can always be forgiven.

## SUMMARY
The chief priests are determined to arrest Jesus, but because of the crowds, they need help from someone on the inside of Jesus' circle of disciples. That help arrives in the form of Judas Iscariot (22 v 1-6). But this is of no surprise to Jesus (v 21-22)—as he explains to his disciples, what is about to happen is due to God's plan, not to his lack of control (v 14-20, 37).

Yet this does not make it easy. Jesus' prayer on the Mount of Olives paints a picture of him in agony. His physical body and human nature can barely endure the prospect of what is to come, and yet he is willing to give everything in order to do his Father's will (v 39-44).

Having been arrested, Jesus is then deserted and mocked. Even Peter fails to follow through on his assurances that he will stay loyal to his Lord, and ends up weeping bitterly over his failure (v 33-34, 54-62). The guards taunt Jesus; the religious leaders set up a show trial to condemn him.

Only Jesus maintains his credibility and speaks truth. He is the Son of Man, the Son of God, who will reign in glory and return to judge (v 69-70)—and so, in a sense, it is everyone else who is on trial. And they all fail, as do we—which makes the account

of the Son of Man's determination to go to the cross to win forgiveness for Peter and all Jesus' flawed people all the more precious.

Ensure in this study that your group do not only understand the passage, but react to it. We should not read of these events without feeling and responding—do pause where appropriate to pray in deep gratitude for the love of the Lord Jesus for you.

## OPTIONAL EXTRA
Either before or after the session, and in light of Jesus' refusal to obscure the truth in his trial while Peter denied the truth outside, source a list of countries where Christians face persecution or imprisonment for standing publicly as believers in Jesus—the websites of Open Doors and the Barnabas Fund are good places to find such information. Spend time praying that the Lord would strengthen these believers to stand and point them to his forgiveness if and when they fail.

## GUIDANCE FOR QUESTIONS
**1. Have you ever stood up for someone, or for the truth, even though you knew it was risky? What caused you to take that stand?**
- **Have you ever let someone down badly? What caused you to do so? Were you able to repair the relationship—and if so, how?**

In order to limit the length of time you spend on this question, you could ask your group to write down their answers before sharing some of them together. Aim to have your own answer prepared, in case the group cannot think of examples from their own lives. You could return to this after Q8 and Q12. Jesus stood up for the truth and walked toward the cross where he would die for his people. Peter lets Jesus down at the exact same time, catastrophically. And it meant that he needed, more than ever, the Lord's forgiveness and restoration of him.

**2. What is shocking about:**

• **Judas' actions (v 4-6, 21-22)?** Judas betrays his friend to death—and greed appears to be at least part of his motivation. Notice that, although Judas is acting under the influence of Satan (v 3), Jesus makes clear in v 22 that Judas is responsible for his own actions.

• **Jesus' words about the Passover meal (v 14-20)?** This meal was one of reverent celebration of a past event—God's rescue of his people from Egypt. Yet here, the meal is overshadowed by Jesus' statement that his suffering is imminent (v 15); it is marked by a sense that something is coming to an end. Jesus will not eat this meal again until the kingdom has come (v 16-18); and Jesus redefines this meal as being about his body broken and his blood shed, rather than about the death of the lambs in Egypt. Jesus is declaring that his upcoming death is the greater final act of salvation by God. Remembering the Passover in Egypt will now be replaced by remembering the greater sacrifice of the true Passover lamb—Jesus.

• **the disciples' priorities (v 24)?** Perhaps prompted by a debate about which of them was the worst and would betray Jesus (v 23), the disciples end up debating which of them is the greatest. In the context of Jesus speaking of his own suffering and death, what a terrible subject for them to turn to!

• **Jesus' statements about the disciples**

**and about himself (v 31-37)?**
**Note:** "you" in v 31 is plural—Jesus is speaking to Simon Peter as the leader of the disciples, but he is speaking about all the disciples.

Satan has demanded to sift the disciples—sifting involves a violent shaking, and the events of the next 24 hours will be a terrible test for the disciples.

Not only that, but Jesus knows that Peter will deny him three times (v 34). Peter is confident in himself (v 33); but Jesus knows him better than he knows himself. The shock is that Peter, even Peter, will not stand the test.

Meanwhile, Jesus is also facing his greatest trial. The prophecies of the suffering servant (v 37) are about to be fulfilled in him. The Son of God will be numbered among the condemned criminals.

**3. What do verses 25-26 teach us about a Christian view of greatness?** In the economy of Christ's kingdom, great people act as if they were the person who is the youngest (and thus, least worthy of honor); the one who rules should be like the one who waits tables (v 26).

• **How do the example of Jesus (v 27) and the gift of Jesus (v 29-30) help us to obey this teaching of Jesus?** *Jesus' example (v 27):* If a server is not greater than the person he waits upon at the table, then (by implication) the disciples are not greater than Jesus their master. And if Jesus' conduct "among them" has been "as one who serves," how can his disciples possibly be obsessed with whether or not they appear great to others?
*Jesus' gift (v 29-30):* Jesus gives us a place in his kingdom, and a role of authority within it. We do not need to seek praise or seize positions of greatness in this life. We have been given far more for the next.

**4. Read Isaiah 51 v 17 and Jeremiah 25 v 15-16. What is "the cup" (Luke 22 v 42) that Jesus asks his Father to remove?** The prophets sometimes spoke of God's wrath and judgment against sin as a cup that the wicked were required to drink. The cup is symbolic, representing the fury, anger, and punishment of God. To put it simply, the cup that Jesus prays about is full of God's perfect and holy hatred for sin.

- **What is astonishing about the second half of verse 42?** It is understandable that Jesus asked his Father to remove the cup. It is astounding that he was so determined to do his Father's will that he was willing to drink the cup anyway, even though it would cost him everything.

**5. How do verses 41-44 make you feel?** Encourage your group to give one-word answers. There are lots of good answers. Members may feel awe-struck, sad, repentant, grateful, loved, etc. Really, the purpose of this question is to ensure that we do not read these verses and feel nothing.

**6. APPLY: How does the account of Jesus on the Mount of Olives show you:**
- **what love is?** Love is being willing to do whatever it takes, at whatever cost to the lover, in order to bring blessing and honor to the beloved. Jesus faced and took the cup because he loved his people and loved his Father.

- **how loved God's people are?** If just a taste—just the anticipation—of God's wrath, was enough to make Jesus fall to the ground and sweat drops of blood, how much worse was his actual experience at his crucifixion? But so great was Jesus' love for his Father and for us that he went willingly to the cross, knowing what he would experience there.

You may well want to stop and pray at this point.

**7. Who mistreats Jesus in these harrowing scenes [in v 47-71], and how?**
- v 47-48: Judas, one of the chosen disciples, uses a form of intimate, friendly greeting to betray his friend and master.
- v 54-60: Peter denies, repeatedly, any knowledge of his Lord. For all his bluster about how he would die for Jesus (v 33), Peter crumples in the face of a slave girl and two strangers. At Jesus' moment of greatest distress, his friend denies ever knowing him. He chooses his own safety over his loyalty to Jesus.
- v 63-65: The guards hurl insults and inflict pain on this pathetic criminal, unaware that this is also their Maker.
- v 66-71: The ruling council put the Son of Man on trial for his life, and find him guilty (v 71) when he tells the truth about his identity (v 69-70). They dare to sit in judgment over the Son of Man, and never pause to consider that he may be telling them the truth.

**8. What does Peter claim about himself (v 55-60)?** That he does not know Jesus. This is not a one-off failure, quickly corrected; his three denials show us a settled determination to distance himself from Jesus. He lies.

- **What does Jesus claim about himself (v 69-70—see Daniel 7 v 13-14)?** That he is the divine Son of Man from Daniel 7 v 13-14—and that after his crucifixion, resurrection, and ascension, he "will be seated at the right hand of the mighty God" (Luke 22 v 69). He also fails to contradict the idea that he is the Son of God (v 70)—effectively, his answer affirms that he agrees with the idea that he is God's Son. This (assuming that you were not telling the truth) was blasphemy, which was punishable by death.

**9. Who is really on trial in all these overnight events?** Everyone!

• The disciples are being sifted.

• The religious leaders are making the final decision whether to humbly accept Jesus' claims and rule, or whether to condemn him for blasphemy.

• Jesus is, of course, on trial, for his life—he must choose whether to tell the truth about himself and walk toward the cross, or obscure the truth in order to save himself.

• **Who comes through their trial with their credibility intact?** Only Jesus. **Who loses theirs?** Everyone else. The disciples disappear after v 53, apart from Peter, who fails his trial by the fire, denying Jesus. The religious leaders, who claim to represent God and serve him, end up rigging a show trial which condemns God's Son to death.

**EXPLORE MORE**
**Read Philippians 2 v 6-11. Where on that timeline [of the incarnation, death, ascension and exaltation of God the Son] do the events of Luke 22 take place?** Between his incarnation and death. **What is to follow (Philippians 2 v 8-11)?**

• Jesus' death on a cross, in obedience to his Father.

• Jesus' exaltation by his Father to the supreme position in the cosmos.

• Every knee bowing before Jesus and every tongue recognizing Jesus as Lord.

**Who will recognize Jesus as Lord at the final trial?** Everyone. No one—including the religious leaders—will deny Jesus' identity as Son of Man, and his right to rule, on the final day.

**Note:** This does not mean they will repent and be saved. It simply means that they will have to recognize his authority as they stand before him in judgment.

**How do you think knowing this truth, as he did (Luke 22 v 69), strengthened Jesus to tell the truth at his trial and walk toward death on his cross?** Because he could look through his suffering to his exaltation. He knew that glory would follow. It is the same for his people (see Romans 8 v 18).

**10. Do you think Simon Peter overreacts to his failures in verses 61-62? Why / why not?** The obvious answer is "no." He was correct to weep bitterly over his own terrible sin in denying Jesus at the moment that Jesus was on trial for his life. But this should prompt the follow-up question: if Peter's failure to be loyal to Jesus should drive him to weep, should not ours too? If we have ever remained silent when we should have spoken up for Jesus, or if we have ever hidden what we really believe so that people will not reject us, then we are not so different from Peter. If we think Simon Peter is not overreacting, then we should also be willing to accept the seriousness of our sin and weep over it.

• **Why is there still hope for him (v 32—see 24 v 33-36)?** In the end Peter was restored, just as Jesus had predicted back in verse 32. The risen Jesus appeared to Peter. Luke does not tell us what he said to him—but Peter was given the privilege of seeing the risen Lord. Not only this, but Peter was present with the other disciples to hear Jesus proclaim, "Peace" (24 v 36). While Peter was backing away from Jesus, Jesus was walking forward to the cross in order to die for Peter's sin. Because of that, there was hope and restoration for Peter.

**11. APPLY: What difference would it make to Jesus' identity if no one in the world believes he is the Son of Man?** None! God condescends to allow everyone to pass judgment on him. But Jesus is the Son of Man whether or not anyone chooses to acknowledge that reality.

• **How should that affect how we live in this world?** We can live obeying Jesus confidently. Even if we are the only person in a room who accepts who Jesus is, he is still truly the Son of Man, who will return in power and bring salvation and judgment. The opinion of people does not affect the truth in any way.

**12. APPLY: How has reading about the events of the night before Jesus' death motivated you to be publicly loyal to him?** Hopefully, Jesus' love seen on the Mount of Olives has drawn out a grateful desire to love him in return; Peter's failure has inspired a determination to stand for Jesus ourselves; Jesus' bravery has prompted a prayer that the Spirit might give us the same bravery; and Jesus' forgiveness and restoration have freed us to repent and walk forward once more. Point out to your group that though they should leave motivated to live for Jesus in their lives and stand for him, they will fail at some point—so encourage them to finish by reading the Getting Personal after this question. The purpose of Luke's account of these events is not so much to cause us to do better, but to help us more deeply enjoy the love and forgiveness of Jesus when we don't do better.

# 7 Luke 23 v 1-47
# OPENING THE KINGDOM

## THE BIG IDEA
Jesus died to bear God's judgment that we deserve for rejecting him, so that the way into his kingdom is open, and we can live with him forever.

## SUMMARY
This study takes your group from the trial before Pilate, along the path to the cross, and then to Jesus' final breath. The events will be familiar:

• Pilate's failure to do what is right, and his choice to do what is easiest, condemning Jesus to death

• The crowd's choice of a murderer to be freed so that God's King will be gone from their midst

• Jesus' promise to one of the criminals dying next to him that he will respond to the criminal's request to be remembered by bringing him into his kingdom to live with him forever

• The darkness overhead, signifying God's anger at human sin—and the human Son of God's death in that darkness

• The tearing of the temple curtain, which had divided the place of God's presence from the people

As with the last study, pray that your group will feel these events, rather than merely understanding them. There may be no new insights as such for your group if they are as familiar with the passage as many Christians are—but there should be deep, awe-struck gratitude that the Son of God should condescend to be tried and executed by the people he made, so that he could bear God's wrath at their sin and open the way into his eternal kingdom.

## OPTIONAL EXTRA

Jesus' final words are full of confidence and trust—as ours can be too. But some final words are hilarious. Ask group members to find and bring their favorites, or google "funny last words" and share those.

## GUIDANCE FOR QUESTIONS

**1. What would you say are the most important turning points in history?** Don't let this discussion continue too long. There is no right or wrong answer—though you could return to it at the end of the study and ask, "How is the day of Jesus' crucifixion an important turning point in history? Would you say it is the most important?"

**2. What does Pilate, the Roman governor, know (v 4, 15, 22)?** That Jesus presents no immediate threat to Rome's rule, and has done nothing wrong. It is important to remember that Pilate is absolutely convinced that Jesus is innocent; otherwise, nothing that follows will seem quite as horrible as it should.

• **What does Pilate do (v 24-25)?** He opts to release Barabbas (this study goes into more detail on that in Q3-4); he "surrendered Jesus to their will." In other words, Pilate caves in to the desires of the mob and hands Jesus over to an execution he knows Jesus did not deserve. **Why, do you think?** Pilate appears to fear the crowd. He does what is easy rather than what is right.

**3. How does the crowd respond to Pilate's desire to release Jesus (v 18, 21, 23)?** They ask for Jesus to be done away with (v 18). They scream for his crucifixion (v 21). They insist and demand that Jesus be killed (v 23).

• **Who would they rather have as part of their society than the Lord Jesus (v 18-19)?** Barabbas, who is a rebel and a murderer.

**4. What did Barabbas face at the start of the day, and at the end of the day?** At the start of the day Barabbas was sitting in a Roman jail awaiting a certain death and the most gruesome form of execution imaginable. But when the guard came to get him, instead of placing a cross on his back, he unlocked his shackles and set him free. At the end of the day he was enjoying freedom and life. **Why?** Because another man was being crucified instead. Barabbas, the guilty man, went free and Jesus, the innocent one, died as a criminal.

### EXPLORE MORE

**When the women following Jesus mourned for him, what did Jesus tell them to do (v 28)?** Not to weep for him, but to weep for themselves and their children.

**Why should they do this (v 29-30)?** Because a day is coming that will be so terrible that the social stigma of barrenness will be preferable to enduring that day while trying to care for a child, and when it would be better to have a mountain collapse on you than to live through it.

**Read Luke 21 v 20-24. What is Jesus saying the women should save their mourning for?** As your group saw in Study Five, the catastrophe of the fall of Jerusalem (which took place in AD 70) is what Jesus knew was coming toward the city. In a similar way to how the northern kingdom was destroyed in 722 BC, so now Jerusalem would be destroyed with cruelty and violence. **Read Revelation 6 v 12-17. What else is Jesus telling them to save their mourning for?** God's day of final judgment will be another terrible day, when many would rather be buried under a mountain than have to face their Creator. Jesus is experiencing God's judgment as he walks towards his cross and his death. But he is not the only condemned human in this scene. The others will also experience this judgment, unless they accept the forgiveness that God's Son offers through his death (see Luke 23 v 34).

**5. APPLY: How do we see the crowd's decision being made in our own lives, and in our society?** *In our own lives:* When we sin, it's a kind of temporary insanity! We are imagining that we would be happier with the experience and effects of sin than with the presence and blessing of obeying Jesus. When we sin, we are acting as though Jesus did not exist; wishing that he were not the living King. We are shouting what the crowd did. Sin is not a brief slip or an excusable mistake. It is shouting, "Away with this man" at King Jesus.
*In our society:* Anytime we choose to reject God's standards for justice, moral conduct, gender, race relations, treatment of the poor, etc., we are choosing to embrace all kinds of societal decay, violence and injustice. We cannot turn away from Jesus' rule without releasing some form of chaos or injustice; just as the crowd not only chose to reject Jesus, but to free Barabbas, a murderer, to live and act in their midst.

• **Read 1 Peter 3 v 18; Colossians 1 v 21-22; Revelation 1 v 5b. How are we like Barabbas?** You and I were

sinners; we sat in a spiritual prison, bound helpless, awaiting the day when we would get the just punishment that we deserve. But then Jesus gwent off to the cross in our place. He got what we deserve; we get what he deserves.

**6. How do the two criminals crucified with Jesus respond to him?**
• **v 39:** The first criminal rails against Jesus, parroting the words of the crowds (v 35 and v 37) and calling on Jesus—if he really is the all-powerful Messiah—to save himself and them. He means, of course, that if Jesus is really the King, he should get himself and these criminals off their crosses.

• **v 40-42:** The second criminal recognizes that:
  • Jesus is an innocent man.
  • The justice of God lays behind his suffering—he is "punished justly" according to his deeds (v 41).
  • Jesus can help him, not by getting him off his cross but in giving him life beyond his death (v 42).

**7. So what is remarkable about Jesus' words in verse 43?** Jesus promises such a man that he will be in paradise—perfection, a return to Eden-like life—that same day. Don't miss the force of this: such a man—a hardened, condemned criminal—is able to live in paradise forever, all because of Jesus.

• **In what sense are "with me" the most exciting part of this promise?** Because the thief will get to be with Jesus forever. It is a reminder that being with Jesus is the definition of paradise! The thing that makes paradise so wonderful is the presence of Jesus. It's not primarily paradise because there are a lot of fun things to do and see. It's not paradise primarily because the problems that plague you here on earth are behind you. It's paradise because we will be with Jesus (see Philippians 1 v 23; 2 Corinthians 5 v 6). He is the greatest reward.

**8. Read Joel 2 v 1-2 and Amos 5 v 18-20. What does the darkness in the middle of the day (Luke 23 v 44-45) signify?** The judgment of God—his wrath at human sin.

**9. What two things happen in the darkness?**
• **v 45:** The curtain in the temple tears. The Gospel writers do not specify which of the many curtains in the temple was torn, but the most theologically significant one was the curtain that hung around the presence of God in the Most Holy Place.
• **v 46:** Jesus dies.

**10. Read Genesis 3 v 23-24 and Exodus 26 v 30-34. What did the curtain in the temple represent?** The separation between humanity and the perfect presence of God. When humans sinned, they were banished from Eden, and cherubim—angels—with flashing swords barred the way back in. The cherubim embroidered on the temple curtain around the Most Holy Place made the link back to Eden. There was no way for humanity to enter and enjoy unrestricted access to God's presence and the perfection of life there.

**11. Explain what Jesus' death achieved, using the events of verses 44-45a, 45b, and 46.** Encourage your group to write down their answers before sharing them, so that they use their own words. By bearing God's just wrath over sin and the punishment of death on the cross, Jesus was the sufficient and one sacrifice required for that sin—our sin. This achievement was

symbolized by the tearing of the curtain, showing that the way to eternity in God's presence, God's kingdom, is now opened.

⊻

• **Now use the events in these verses to explain why Jesus died, but imagining that you are speaking with a non-Christian who has never been to church.**

**12. APPLY: How will Christians view death, and why?** In the same way as Jesus did. Death need hold no fear for the Christian, because Jesus has died in our place, experiencing God's judgment in our place so that we, like him, can enter God's presence beyond our death. We can peacefully and confidently commit our spirit into our Father's hands, because his Son, our Savior, has already taken the judgment due to us for our sin.

# 8 Luke 23 v 48 – 24 v 53
# REMEMBER HOW HE TOLD YOU

## THE BIG IDEA

The resurrection of Jesus from the dead—assures us that his promises can be relied on completely; means that by faith, we are at peace with God; and calls us to be part of his mission joyfully to share the gospel of repentance and forgiveness in his name.

## SUMMARY

Again, these events will be familiar to many groups. This study aims to highlight the particular emphases of Luke's account of the burial and resurrection—and, in this Gospel, the ascension—of Jesus:

*The burial of Jesus* (23 v 48-56) is not an afterthought, but an integral part of the story, establishing that the body that rose from the grave is the same one that was placed in the tomb; and giving us a picture of real discipleship, as the women follow Jesus and seek to care for his body, and Joseph risks his position and safety to identify with his King.

*The empty tomb of Jesus* (24 v 1-8) is a remarkably spare account, given its significance! But Luke's goal is first to establish its historicity (see next paragraph), and also to point to the need to listen to heaven's explanation of the facts of the empty tomb—"He has risen!" (v 6); and second to point to the resurrection as the greatest assurance that Jesus keeps his promises. As Christians, we are called to trust Jesus' promises utterly—to "remember how he told" us, and live accordingly. The resurrection proves that we are wise to do so.

*The appearances of Jesus* (v 9-49) establish the reality of Jesus' bodily resurrection, as it was experienced by men who at first found the whole notion "nonsense" (v 11). The appearances also point us to where we can meet with Jesus and be made confident of the truth of his resurrection—to the Scriptures, as Jesus opens our eyes to it (v 25-27, 44-45).

*The ascension of Jesus* (v 46-53) is a fitting finale—Jesus is enthroned in heaven, and his people await the indwelling of his Spirit to empower them to preach the gospel joyfully. Luke's Gospel began in the temple with news of joy and gladness (1 v 14); and it ends with Jesus' forgiven subjects praising God joyfully in that same temple. No other responses other than worship, praise and joy are appropriate for those who have been given certainty about the birth, life, death, resurrection, and ascension of Christ Jesus.

## OPTIONAL EXTRA

To link to the fact that the resurrection of Jesus, which he had promised several times before his death, proves that his word can be trusted, perform a trust exercise, such as that where someone lets themselves fall backwards, trusting that someone standing behind them will catch them. Some people simply cannot bring themselves to let themselves fall, no matter how many times their partner promises to catch them!

## GUIDANCE FOR QUESTIONS

**1. What has been the greatest positive surprise of your life?**

- **Did that positive surprise change the way you were feeling in any way? How?**

This final section of Luke is one of wonderful surprise—the women arriving at the tomb to be told that the man they knew was dead is alive; the two disciples on the road to Emmaus discovering they had been walking with Jesus for hours; the disciples gathered in the room meeting the risen Jesus. And these surprises prompted a desire to share the news, and feelings of burning hearts and of joy. So as you share your stories in this question, enjoy the surprises and think hard about their emotional impact; and then you could return to this after Q3, 8 and/or 9.

**2. How do the women (v 49, 55-56) and Joseph (v 50-54) give us a picture of what real discipleship involves?**

- *The women:* They are with Jesus to the end. The men are not mentioned after 22 v 62. The women stick with Jesus as he dies (23 v 49) and is buried (v 55-56). They remain faithful when it is hard to do so.
- *Joseph:* Joseph had a prominent position as a member of the Council. He had much to lose. But he chose to identify himself publicly with Jesus (see 9 v 26). While some others watched from a distance, he moved toward Jesus in an act of devotion and care. Joseph loved Jesus even when it was not clear what good it could possibly accomplish. This is real discipleship.

**3. What facts confront them [the women] (24 v 2-3)?** The huge stone that sealed the tomb's entrance had been rolled away (v 2) and there was no body in the tomb to be found (v 3).

- **Who provides an explanation for those facts (v 4-5)?** Two "men" in shining clothing standing there at the entrance to the tomb. Clearly, these were

men in appearance only, for "their clothes gleamed like lightning" (v 4). They were angels, and the women bowed down before them in fear (v 5—this is a common response to the appearance of an angel; see 1 v 12, 29-30) (For more on angels, see Explore More section after Q11). **And what is that explanation (v 6)?** "He is not here; he has risen!" Note that it requires heaven's explanation to rightly interpret the evidence of the empty tomb. Peter had no such assistance (v 12) and was left wondering, rather than understanding.

**4. In a sense the women should not have been surprised by what they found. Why not (v 6-7)?** The substance of the angelic message was an encouragement to the women to remember the words that Jesus had already spoken to them in advance about all that had just happened (v 6-7; see 9 v 22 and 18 v 32-33). He had told them that he would die… and that he would rise. The women allowed the seemingly insurmountable circumstances in front of them to overwhelm the memory of what Jesus had told them would happen. But if they had remembered and trusted Jesus' promises, they would have expected him to rise from the dead.

**5. What does the empty tomb tell them, and us, about Jesus' promises?** His word is always true and what he says will happen always comes to pass. His promises are utterly trustworthy.

**6. What has Jesus promised us?**
- **6 v 22-23:** We will be rejected and insulted on account of our faith—but we are also blessed.
- **9 v 24:** We are called to lose our lives for the sake of the gospel—and we will save

our eternal lives in so doing.

- **11 v 13:** God gives us the Holy Spirit.
- **11 v 28:** Blessing is found in obeying God's word.
- **12 v 4-8:** We have nothing to fear in death, for we are known and valued by the One who has power over our eternal destiny. If we stand publicly for Jesus today, he will stand and affirm us as his subjects on the final day.
- **12 v 40; 17 v 22-24:** Jesus is coming back—and we won't miss it.
- **18 v 29-30:** Whatever you give up to follow Christ—and following Christ will mean giving up much—you will receive far more in this life, and infinitely more in the next.

**7. APPLY: Which of these promises do you find hardest to believe and act upon? How does trusting it give greater joy and security in life?** Different people will have different answers. Encourage your group not to excuse a lack of belief in themselves (or each other). But it is often those promises that we find hardest to believe and live out that are those that will bring us most joy as we do so.

**8. What does Jesus do to change their minds about the claims of the women (v 13-45)?**

- v 25-27 (and v 44): He explained to them that God's chosen King was destined to suffer and to then enter his glory, and that this was all laid out throughout the Old Testament. Every part of the Old Testament pointed forward to or prepared God's people for the King who would come to die and rise again for his people. All of the people and patterns and prophecies of the Old Testament find their

fulfillment in the death and resurrection of Jesus. And so the Scriptures show that something like what the women claimed is what the disciples should have been expecting.

- v 35: Jesus opened their "eyes" to be able to recognize him as the risen Jesus (and, later in v 45, to understand his word).
- v 34-36: Jesus appeared to different groups of his followers at different times. This was no one-off vision or hallucination.
- v 39-41, 42-43: Jesus' body was physical— it could be touched, and he could eat. And it was definitely him—the reference to "his hands and feet" is presumably because those displayed the nail wounds from the cross.

⌄

- **What did it take for them to realize that Jesus really had risen (v 31, 45—see v 16)?** It required Jesus to work in them to open their eyes/minds. Without that work of his in them, they would still have been kept from seeing him (v 16). We cannot figure this out ourselves. We need Jesus' work in us to reveal it to us.

**9. Why are Jesus' first words to his gathered disciples in verse 36 surprising, and wonderful? (Hint: Think about the disciples' performance over the previous few days.)** Explain to your group that the concept of peace—the Hebrew word is *shalom*—was significant to the Jewish way of thinking; it implied wholeness, harmony, and prosperity—a return to life in Eden. So it is wonderful that the crucified, risen Jesus is able to offer this "peace." And it is surprising (and wonderful!) that the risen Jesus would grant this peace to such flawed, failing followers as were gathered in that room—and to us. Jesus knows that we let him down and fail to obey or stand for him—yet he still says, "Peace be with you."

**10. We do not have the risen Jesus standing in front of us, but we do have the Scriptures, including Moses and all the prophets. Why is this wonderful for us (v 25-27, 44-49)?** Because those Scriptures tell us all we need to know. When Jesus was physically present with his people, he still pointed them to the Scriptures as the place where they would find an explanation of what had taken place, and an outline of their role in the story of God's work in the world (v 47-49). It was the Scriptures he opened their minds to understand (v 45). We cannot see Jesus; but we can still meet with him in all his word, just as they could.

**11. What is the mission of the church (v 47-49, 52-53)?**

• v 47-48: To witness to the truth that we know about Jesus the Messiah, and to hold out his command to repent and his offer of forgiveness.

• v 49: To conduct this mission relying on his power (the Holy Spirit), and not on our own.

• v 52-53: Together to worship Jesus, and to praise God joyfully.

**EXPLORE MORE**
**How do the events of the end of Luke's Gospel remind us of the events of the beginning of Luke's Gospel?**
**Read 1 v 8-13, 26-28 and 2 v 8-9; link to 24 v 4-5:** Angels are present at both the beginning and end of the Gospel, announcing truth and explaining events.
**Read 1 v 7, 13, 31, 34; link to 24 v 1, 3, 5-6:** There is life in a place where life is impossible: a barren womb, a virgin's womb, and a tomb.
**Read 1 v 37; link to 24 v 6b-8:** God's

word does not fail: so his promise that Mary would conceive was to be trusted, and his promise that he would die and rise should have been trusted.
**Read 1 v 46-47 and 2 v 8-10; link to 24 v 52-53:** Understanding who Jesus is and living under his rule causes us to rejoice and praise God.
**Read 2 v 8-11; link to 24 v 46-47:** Christ came, and died and rose, to be our Savior, offering forgiveness to all who repent. This is the "good news"—the gospel.

**12. APPLY: How has Luke's Gospel prompted you to worship Jesus with great joy? Which truths and insights from Luke 12 – 24 have particularly struck you?** Encourage your group to write their answer(s) down in the space provided before they share them with the others. If you have worked through the Good Book Guide to Luke 1 – 12 before this one, then encourage your group to think back throughout the whole Gospel. The aim of this question is to sum up the whole series of studies simply by enjoying what you have seen of the Lord Jesus, and worshiping him for who he is.

# Good Book Guides
## The full range

**Ephesians:** 8 Studies
Richard Coekin
ISBN: 9781910307694

**Philippians:** 7 Studies
Steven J. Lawson
ISBN: 9781784981181

**Colossians:** 6 Studies
Mark Meynell
ISBN: 9781906334246

**1 Thessalonians:**
7 Studies
Mark Wallace
ISBN: 9781904889533

**2 Timothy:** 7 Studies
Mark Mulryne
ISBN: 9781905564569

**Titus:** 5 Studies
Tim Chester
ISBN: 9781909919631

**Hebrews:** 8 Studies
Justin Buzzard
ISBN: 9781906334420

**James:** 6 Studies
Sam Allberry
ISBN: 9781910307816

**1 Peter:** 5 Studies
Tim Chester
ISBN: 9781907377853

**1 Peter:** 6 Studies
Juan R. Sanchez
ISBN: 9781784980177

**1 John:** 7 Studies
Nathan Buttery
ISBN: 9781904889953

**Revelation 2–3:** 7 Studies
Jonathan Lamb
ISBN: 9781905564682

### TOPICAL

**Man of God:** 10 Studies
Anthony Bewes & Sam
Allberry
ISBN: 9781904889977

**Biblical Womanhood:**
10 Studies
Sarah Collins
ISBN: 9781907377532

**The Apostles' Creed:**
10 Studies
Tim Chester
ISBN: 9781905564415

**Promises Kept Bible
Overview:** 9 Studies
Carl Laferton
ISBN: 9781908317933

**Contentment:** 6 Studies
Anne Woodcock
ISBN: 9781905564668

**These truths alone: the
Reformation Solas**
6 Studies
Jason Helopoulos
ISBN: 9781784981501

**Women of Faith:**
8 Studies
Mary Davis
ISBN: 9781904889526

**Meeting Jesus:** 8 Studies
Jenna Kavonic
ISBN: 9781905564460

**Heaven:** 6 Studies
Andy Telfer
ISBN: 9781909919457

**Making Work Work:**
8 Studies
Marcus Nodder
ISBN: 9781908762894

**The Holy Spirit:** 8 Studies
Pete & Anne Woodcock
ISBN: 9781905564217

**Experiencing God:**
6 Studies
Tim Chester
ISBN: 9781906334437

**Real Prayer:** 7 Studies
Anne Woodcock
ISBN: 9781910307595

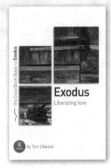

# thegoodbook

COMPANY

*Opening up the Bible*

At The Good Book Company, we are dedicated to helping Christians and local churches grow. We believe that God's growth process always starts with hearing clearly what he has said to us through his timeless word—the Bible.

Ever since we opened our doors in 1991, we have been striving to produce resources that honor God in the way the Bible is used. We have grown to become an international provider of user-friendly resources to the Christian community, with believers of all backgrounds and denominations using our Bible studies, books, evangelistic resources, DVD-based courses and training events.

We want to equip ordinary Christians to live for Christ day by day, and churches to grow in their knowledge of God, their love for one another, and the effectiveness of their outreach.

Call us for a discussion of your needs or visit one of our local websites for more information on the resources and services we provide.

Your friends at The Good Book Company

---

**NORTH AMERICA**
**UK & EUROPE**
**AUSTRALIA**
**NEW ZEALAND**

thegoodbook.com
thegoodbook.co.uk
thegoodbook.com.au
thegoodbook.co.nz

866 244 2165
0333 123 0880
(02) 9564 3555
(+64) 3 3343 2463

**WWW.CHRISTIANITYEXPLORED.ORG**
Our partner site is a great place for those exploring the Christian faith, with a clear explanation of the good news, powerful testimonies and answers to difficult questions.